JUVENILE OFFENDERS BEFORE THE COURTS

JUVENILE OFFENDERS BEFORE THE COURTS

BY

MAX GRÜNHUT

READER IN CRIMINOLOGY IN THE
UNIVERSITY OF OXFORD

GREENWOOD PRESS, PUBLISHERS
WESTPORT, CONNECTICUT

Library of Congress Cataloging in Publication Data

Grünhut, Max, 1893-1964.
Juvenile offenders before the courts.

Reprint of the 1956 ed. published by the Clarendon Press, Oxford.
Includes index.
1. Juvenile delinquency--Great Britain. 2. Juvenile courts--Great Britain. I. Title.
[KD8471.G73 1978] 345'.41'08 77-27073
ISBN 0-313-20194-3

This reprint has been authorized by the Clarendon Press, Oxford

Reprinted in 1978 by Greenwood Press, Inc.,
51 Riverside Avenue
Westport, CT. 06880

Printed in the United States of America

10 9 8 7 6 5 4 3 2 1

PREFACE

MODERN criminology has accumulated a considerable amount of empirical knowledge about the personal circumstances and social background of juvenile delinquents. More recently the emphasis has shifted from the search for causes of crime to investigations of the effects of various forms of penal and correctional treatment. All such studies are undertaken in the hope of providing some help and guidance to the courts in the selection of the right form of treatment for the individual offender. We know, however, very little about the present sentencing practice of the courts in various parts of the country and the way they deal with different crime situations confronting the magistrates in their particular districts. There is no doubt that much valuable experience has been gained in the local sphere which should be brought to light for the mutual benefit of the courts and the advancement of criminological knowledge.

The present survey of juvenile delinquency and the treatment practice of the courts in different areas of England and Wales is an attempt to fill this gap. It is the result of research which has been going on for some time with the support of the Home Office and the University of Oxford Social Studies Board. Criminological research usually depends on team-work, and this study, too, had to rely on the co-operation of research workers from many quarters. Miss M. Grain prepared the first basic tables. Throughout all further stages of the work Mrs. S. McCabe acted as Research Assistant. She performed most of the statistical calculations, designed the tables, and made many contributions to the research plan and the presentation of the results. In more complicated statistical questions expert advice was generously forthcoming. Dr. Frank Burchardt, Director of the Oxford Institute of Statistics, took a kind interest in the preparation of the scheme. Whenever new difficulties arose and threatened to bar progress, Mr. T. S. Lodge, Statistical Adviser to the Home Office, was ready to give the work the benefit of his advice and help. When it came to the final question of a statistical analysis of the results of different treatment policies on different types of offenders in different localities, Mr. L. T. Wilkins, Senior Research Officer of the Social Survey, was kind enough to undertake himself the statistical calculations which form the basis of discussion in the fourth chapter. The field-work which provided the data for this part was carried out by Mrs. A. Horridge, Mr. D. Schub, and Mr. W. H. Beacham. Miss M. Potter, of the Oxford University School of Geography, designed the maps. Acknowledgement is made to the Controller of H.M. Stationery Office for permission to use the maps on the density of population from the official handbook on Britain for the design of Map 2. Acknowledgement is also made to the Director General of the Ordnance Survey Office for permission to use the 1/625,000 map of Great Britain, sheets 1 and 2, and to the Controller of H.M. Stationery Office for the use of the map of the West Yorkshire conurbation appearing in the Census 1951, One per Cent. Sample Tables, Part II which were taken as a basis for the design of Map 4. Chief Constables, Probation Officers, and Children's Officers very kindly provided information on many details.

Now that the work is finished I wish to extend my grateful thanks to all those who contributed to it by their kind help and co-operation. I also thank most sincerely Mr. C. P. Hill of the Home Office Children's Department, who first suggested that the material made available for this book should be used for criminological purposes and who secured the official support without which it would not have been possible to embark on these studies.

M. G.

Oxford

March 1955

CONTENTS

CHAPTER I

INTRODUCTION

The Work of Juvenile Courts in England and Wales

FEW movements for the reform of the law and the development of social services have succeeded in gaining such universal acceptance as the demand, at the beginning of the present century, for an appropriate machinery for the treatment of delinquent youth. Juvenile courts in Britain, in America, and on the European continent, and Child Welfare Councils in the Scandinavian countries have become recognized features of modern legal systems and of present-day social administration. Their organization, range of jurisdiction, and forms of procedure differ in accordance with the wider framework of the national legal system to which they have had to be adapted, but, whatever their differences, in their essentials all these institutions have much in common. Where there is a juvenile court worthy of the name there is a similar purpose and the same approach. The juvenile offender is no longer seen as a legal category only. Instead, attention is focused on the psychological, educational, and social problems which lie behind the simple fact of a youthful theft or an act of destruction no less than behind the case of a neglected or ill-treated child. A juvenile court, therefore, does not deal with offenders only nor does it award to offenders legal punishments alone. In the course of time these ideas have extended beyond the limits of the penal and corrective treatment of juveniles. In a number of countries the application in modified form of juvenile court methods to the treatment of adolescent offenders, that is minors over juvenile court age, has become a topical subject of recent law reform. Even the treatment of adult criminals has, in the principal approach rather than in legal forms and statutory provisions, been influenced by the experience gained in juvenile courts.

The main idea underlying these tendencies is the principle of individual prevention, the responsibility of the State and the community for the individual delinquent in the sense that it is the primary purpose of his treatment to prevent him from further wrongdoing. However, in the juvenile court this preventive purpose implies more than the mere negative aim of making him avoid further criminal activities. Rather are its efforts directed to the positive end of giving the young delinquent a better start in life, making him a better son to his parents, a more satisfactory pupil in his school, a more successful worker in his employment and occupation, and a man more careful in the choice of his companions. These far-reaching aims cannot be achieved by strictly circumscribed legal precepts; they require a wide discretion on the part of those who are called to administer such a system. The widening of judicial discretion, however, creates a new problem—the conflict between the requirements of uniformity and predictability which are inherent in the idea of law and justice, and the demand for the individualization of treatment. There is no universal answer to the question how these two requirements should be reconciled. One of the consequences of this situation is that the individualization of treatment must find its counterpart in the differentiation of criminological research. It is not sufficient to describe the achievements of the juvenile court movement as a whole or to follow up the effects of the work of the juvenile courts in a particular country as they appear in the columns of the national criminal statistics. The ultimate object of realistic research is the study of the work of individual juvenile courts in order to find out similarities and differences both in the tasks with which the Bench is confronted and in the ways in which magistrates deal with the specific problems before them.

Britain stands among those countries in which pioneer work was done in the establishment of juvenile courts. In English law, the Children Act, 1908, was the first statutory recognition of juvenile courts. After twenty-five years of experience this Act was repealed by the Children and Young Persons Act, 1933, which is the legal foundation of present-day juvenile courts in England and Wales.[1] English juvenile courts are courts of summary jurisdiction. This means that they are primarily courts of criminal jurisdiction which they exert over juvenile offenders between 8 and 17 years of age. They have, however,

[1] 8 Edw. VII (1908), c. 67; 23 Geo. V (1933), c. 12.

a non-criminal jurisdiction over children and young persons who, in a wider sense of the term, are deemed to be 'in need of care or protection'. In the strict statutory meaning this concept refers to two groups only, juveniles who, owing to insufficient parental care, exhibit certain prescribed symptoms of waywardness, and those who are the victims of certain criminal offences committed against them. To these statutory 'care or protection' cases two other groups must be added: juveniles who are regarded by their parents as 'beyond control', and truants. Numerically, the jurisdiction over juvenile offenders plays a much greater part in the work of English juvenile courts than the treatment of non-offenders.

In the last pre-war year, 1938, 61,110 juveniles appeared before magistrates in England and Wales. Out of that number, they found 27,875 guilty of indictable offences and nearly the same number, 27,395, guilty of non-indictable offences. They also took measures in respect of 2,366 non-offenders. Indictment is the written accusation before a court with a jury, either Quarter Sessions or Assizes. Indictable offences are those which are triable before a jury. Some of them must be tried before Quarter Sessions or Assizes. As an outcome of modern legislation many of them are, with the defendant's consent, tried summarily, that is before magistrates' courts. On the whole, indictable offences comprise the more serious crimes, while non-indictable offences which are tried summarily include numerous trifling violations of the law. If one compares the pre-war figures for juveniles appearing before the court with the situation in a typical post-war year, the result is a slight decrease in the number of non-indictable offenders but a drastic increase in both the large number of indictable offenders and the small number of non-offenders. How far a rise or fall in the figures of criminal statistics corresponds to an increase or decrease in actual crime and delinquency is a question which will emerge on several occasions in the course of further discussion. In 1950 the number of children and young persons appearing before the magistrates had risen to 77,052. Out of these, 41,910 were found guilty of indictable offences and 27,125 of non-indictable offences, while the number of non-offenders dealt with by the courts increased to 4,531. These 'care or protection' cases, using the wider sense of this term, while numerically still a small fraction of the work of the juvenile courts, have gained some ground within the administration of juvenile court law. Among every 1,000 juveniles appearing before the magistrates, the number of those in need of care and protection increased from 38·7 in 1938 to 58·8 in 1950.

Criminological studies on the extent and typical features of juvenile delinquency are, almost without exception, based on observations on indictable offences. On the whole, the present investigation follows the same method. However, even non-indictable offences are not without significance, both as a symptom of juvenile delinquency and as part of the jurisdiction of juvenile courts. Behind the slightly decreasing total figures for non-indictable offences committed by juveniles, there are characteristic differences in respect of age and sex groups. While the general falling trend of these non-indictable offences is due to a marked decrease among senior boys between 14 and 17 years, the corresponding figures for junior boys, 8–13, and for girls, increased. For the senior boys, between 1938 and 1950 non-indictable assaults decreased by 7 per cent., offences in connexion with pedal cycles by 22·6 per cent., playing games in the street by 33 per cent., and malicious damage by 37 per cent. This notable downward trend is only partially balanced by an increase of 7·3 per cent. in offences connected with motor vehicles and of 57 per cent. in the small number of offences connected with firearms, and also by a doubling of the cases of poaching. At the same time, non-indictable offences committed by junior boys increased by 37·1 per cent., and the number of those committed by girls of 8–17 increased by 27·4 per cent.

These few figures suggest that there are certain characteristic fluctuations in the form and number of non-indictable offences committed by juveniles. In the discussion which follows, however, the term 'juvenile delinquent' has been limited to persons between 8 and 17 years of age found guilty of an indictable offence unless explicit reference is made to non-indictable offences.

It is an essential feature of any juvenile court that the Bench is not bound to the application of strictly prescribed sanctions of a retributive penal system, but has at its disposal a variety of protective and educative measures. In England, three principal ways of dealing with juvenile delinquents are open to the court. First, the magistrates may come to the conclusion that in a particular case the best way would be to take no action at all. In such a case they would discharge the juvenile absolutely or conditionally, to use the terms introduced by the Criminal Justice Act, 1948.[1] Secondly, the magistrates can apply constructive measures and put the juvenile on probation, commit him to the care of a fit person, or send him to an Approved School. Finally, they can resort to punishment and impose a fine or order the culprit's detention in a Remand Home; since 1952, offenders of 14 and over can be committed to a Detention Centre, and, since 1950, those of 12 and over can be sent to an Attendance Centre, as far as facilities for these new measures are available. Within the non-criminal jurisdiction, the court has at its disposal the same constructive measures as for juvenile offenders, that is supervision by a probation officer, committal to the care of a fit person, or committal to an Approved School.

Table I shows, for a typical post-war period, the year 1950, how magistrates in England and Wales made use of these

TABLE I. *Work of the Juvenile Courts dealing with Delinquents an Non-offenders, 1950*

	All juveniles 8–17	*Absolute and conditional discharge*	*Probation and supervision*	*Fit person*	*Approved Schools*	*Punitive detention*	*Fines*	*Otherwise dealt with*
Indictable offences .	41,910	12,585	17,100	607	3,571	866	6,812	369
Non-indictable offences .	27,125	7,534	1,292	13	130	74	17,997	85
Care or protection .	4,531	—	1,849	2,100	582	—	—	—

powers. In more than one case out of every four in which juveniles were found guilty of indictable offences no action was taken. Of the 29,325 cases in which the magistrates came to the conclusion that positive action should be taken, the vast

[1] 11 and 12 Geo. VI (1948), c. 58, s. 7.

majority, that is 21,278 or 72·5 per cent., were dealt with constructively. In most of these cases the courts made use of probation. For juvenile delinquents who had to be removed from the family home, committals to Approved Schools took precedence over fit-person orders. To commit a child or a young person to the care of a fit person is first and foremost a method applied to juveniles 'in need of care or protection'. Nearly every second of the non-offenders is dealt with in this manner and, as a rule, finds his way to a Children's Home or a foster family. The relative importance of the constructive measures for offenders and non-offenders may be illustrated by the fact that, on a three-year basis, 1948–50, out of every 1,000 juveniles put under the supervision of a probation officer 910 were offenders and 90 non-offenders; out of 1,000 committed to the care of a fit person, 215 were offenders and 785 non-offenders, and out of 1,000 committed to Approved Schools, 853 were offenders and only 147 non-offenders. Institutional training in Approved Schools is, however, a typical form of treatment for wayward girls. In 1950 a total of 464 girls of 14–17 years of age went to Approved Schools. Out of these, 167 were offenders who were committed to an Approved School either when they had been found guilty or after a breach of probation. The majority of these senior girls sent to Approved Schools, that is 297 or 64 per cent., were 'in need of care or protection' or 'beyond control'.

In the course of time, not only has the amount of work of the juvenile courts increased, but there has also been a change in their way of dealing with the children and young persons before them. As a preliminary orientation, Table II illustrates the treatment practice of the magistrates in England and Wales by figures showing proportions of the various forms of treatment awarded in one of the years before and one of the years after the war. The first impression is that even in times of apparent increase in the number of juvenile delinquents, the proportion of offenders dismissed without supervision, that is absolutely or conditionally discharged, remained surprisingly constant. It was 30·9 per cent. in 1938 and 29·9 per cent. in 1950. In the treatment of offenders in respect of whom the magistrates had to take action, there appears a significant change of practice. Between 1938 and 1950 the rate of constructive measures applied to cases too serious to be discharged decreased from 88·9 to 72·5, while the rate of punitive measures increased from 9·2 to 26·2. These figures refute the popular criticism that juvenile courts indulge more and more in unjustified leniency.

TABLE II. *Rates of Treatment awarded in 1938 and 1950*

	Percentage rates of Treatment							
	Number of cases dealt with	*Absolute discharge*	*Conditional discharge*	*Probation and supervision*	*Care of fit person*	*Approved Schools*	*Fines*	*Punitive detention and otherwise dealt with*
1938								
Indictable offences	27,875	23·5	7·4	50·8	0·7	9·7	6·0	1·9
Non-indictable offences . .	27,395	39·3	2·8	5·9	*	0·5	51·4	0·1
Care or protection . . .	2,366	—	—	22·9	40·5	36·6	—	—
1950								
Indictable offences	41,910	13·6	16·3	40·8	1·4	8·5	16·2	3·2
Non-indictable offences . .	27,125	19·5	8·2	4·7	*	*	66·3	1·5
Care or protection . . .	4,531	—	—	40·8	46·3	12·9	—	—

* Percentages in these cases are under 0·5.

The high proportion of punitive measures after the war is due to a drastic increase in the number of fines imposed on juvenile offenders. From 1938 to 1950 the number of juvenile offenders guilty of indictable offences too serious to be dismissed increased by 52·4 per cent. but, at the same time, the number of those fined increased by 305 per cent. Shortly after the end of the war the official Criminal Statistics drew attention to the fact that the 'noticeable change in the methods of dealing with those offenders under 17 has been the decrease in the use of probation and the increase in the use of fines'.[1]

The growing resort to fines is also apparent in the field of non-indictable offences. In 1938 and 1950 the percentage of

[1] *Criminal Statistics, England and Wales, 1947*, p. ix.

non-indictable juvenile offenders who were either discharged or fined remained constant. It amounted to 93 in 1938 and 94 in 1950. Within these constant proportions, however, there was a characteristic movement from discharge to fines. While in 1938 42·1 per cent. of juvenile non-indictable offenders were dismissed and 51·4 fined, in 1950 only 27·7 per cent. were discharged and 66·3 per cent. fined. In the non-criminal jurisdiction a different tendency appears. While the rate of fit-person orders remained almost constant, magistrates, faced with a growing number of care and protection cases, made considerably less use of institutional treatment in Approved Schools, and committed more of these wayward juveniles to the supervision of a probation officer.

These figures illustrate, on the strength of pre-war and post-war experience, the work of English juvenile courts. National figures, however, level out regional and local differences. For this reason they are unsuitable as evidence of the flexibility of the system. It has long been a tradition in English law that the judge is bound by the letter of the law in the question of the prisoner's guilt, but enjoys a notable freedom of discretion in the use of his sentencing power. Magistrates in the juvenile court have a similar discretion. They may either abstain from any action, or apply constructive measures, or inflict punishments, and they are expected to make their choice after a full assessment of each case and after taking into account the juvenile's personality, social background, past career, and future prospects. Even when such a comprehensive view is based on well-ascertained facts, their assessment is ultimately determined by a personal judgement. Personal judgements, however, vary and, for this reason, a flexible system, based on discretion, inevitably leads to diversity in the courts' decisions. Even a system with strictly defined legal concepts and a limited range of statutory punishments never achieves complete uniformity. Discretion is always bound to sacrifice equality to the needs of the individual delinquent and is intended to do so. Since value judgements are affected by personal outlook, past experience, and local tradition, there must be even more divergences expected in the work of the English juvenile courts than in the administration of a criminal code of the classical school.

A few years after the Children and Young Persons Act, 1933,

had come into force, attention was drawn to the diversity in the practice of juvenile courts. In her comprehensive study on the work of the English juvenile courts, Miss W. A. Elkin complained of the 'regrettable lack of any common standard'. 'There is such a startling difference in the method followed by different courts', she said, 'that it is obvious that they cannot all be right.'[1] In the years preceding the Second World War when Miss Elkin undertook her investigation, every second juvenile found guilty of an indictable offence was put on probation, but twelve towns used probation for no more than a third of the cases, and among them the percentage for Windsor, Warrington, and Accrington was as low as 6 per cent. The divergences applied not only to the numerical proportion of offenders put on probation, but also to the timing of probation within the offender's criminal career; in some courts frequent dismissals delayed the application of probation, and in others, after repeated attempts at probation, committals to Approved Schools occurred rather late. At the same time, while the rate of fines for juvenile offenders was 6 per cent. for the whole country, at Oldham more than every third offender was fined and nearly every fourth put on probation. These observations seemed to her a challenge to criminological research. 'The experience accumulated by the courts in the course of years is enormous, but it has been allowed to remain inchoate and has never been so organized that it has become available knowledge.'[2]

The present study is intended to meet this challenge. For this purpose an analysis has been made of the returns from the 134 police districts in England and Wales for the years 1948, 1949, and 1950 indicating how magistrates' courts dealt with juvenile offenders found guilty of indictable offences. The investigation extends to four groups of offenders: boys 8–13, boys 14–17, girls 8–13, girls 14–17; and to five types of disposal: absolute discharge, conditional discharge, probation, committal to an Approved School, and fines. From this starting-point the discussion which follows tries to disclose two unknown factors, the volume and structure of juvenile delinquency in the various districts, on the one hand, and the treatment policy of the

[1] W. A. Elkin, *English Juvenile Courts* (1938), pp. 133 and 304.

[2] Ibid., p. 305.

magistrates in the different courts, on the other. While it is the aim of this study to trace diversities in the treatment of juvenile delinquents, it is not assumed that the mere fact of differences in the treatment practice of the courts is something wrong in itself. The human conscience reacts violently when the boundary that divides what is just from what is unjust has been crossed. Within this boundary, however, it cannot be said with the same precision that one, and only one, course is just. As the comparative study of legislation suggests that there is a limited number of solutions to the same social problems, so a wide experience of court practice shows a limited variety in the treatment of similar cases still compatible with the idea of justice. In matters connected with human behaviour, there is no panacea, but rather a moderate range in the choice of approach to the problems of the individual in whose fate there is always something unique within the endless variations of personal character and human destiny. In the administration of justice no experiments are feasible. This makes it desirable to compare the effects of different methods of treatment applied to similar groups of offenders. The results of this study are not intended to criticize outstanding deviations from the average court practice, but to give an impression of the prevailing variety in treatment policy and to present the experience gained by different ways of approach. It is hoped that this will help to make the selection of treatment a conscious choice, and thus in the end deepen the use of judicial discretion which is the essence of juvenile court work.

Since the present survey is based on the experience of the three years 1948, 1949, and 1950, the results can be expected to be unaffected by certain fluctuations which occurred from year to year during the unstable period immediately after the war. The year 1948 was one of the three peak years in juvenile delinquency which, in an unexplained three-year rhythm in 1945, 1948, and 1951, were characteristic of post-war delinquency in England and Wales (Table III). While the first peak of 1945 seemed to be easily explained as a reflection of the immediate aftermath of the war, the recurrent increase in 1948 gave rise to alarm in many quarters. The tide seemed to abate in 1949, and, while again rising in 1950, still remained below the 1948 level, till it reached a new unprecedented peak in 1951.

In view of these facts, a criminological study based on the triennium 1948–50 can be justified as a contribution to the social history of post-war England.

TABLE III. *Numbers of Juvenile Delinquents and Rates of Juvenile Delinquency, 1944–53*

Year	*Number of juvenile delinquents*	*Rate per 1,000*
1944	40,549	7·9
1945	**43,503**	**8·6**
1946	37,088	7·3
1947	35,694	7·0
1948	**44,454**	**8·8**
1949	40,430	8·1
1950	42,415	8·4
1951	**47,473**	**9·2**
1952	45,078	8·6
1953	38,690	7·2

From a methodological point of view, this survey is primarily a statistical study. Within the last decade the study and use of statistics have made tremendous progress. In the refinement of statistical method and the ever-growing extension of statistical research into numerous fields of science as well as into the study of human behaviour, a new era of 'statistical optimism' seems to have dawned, comparable to the time when Quetelet and Guerry laid the foundations of modern criminal statistics. It is the strength of modern statistical research that it recognizes the verification of its results and the critical determination of its limitations to be among its principal objects. In dealing with criminal statistics we are very much aware of the unascertainable and therefore disturbing factor of the 'dark figure', that is the unknown difference between the number of crimes committed and of crimes recorded. The skill of the offender in avoiding detection, the inclination of the public to report crimes and to prosecute offenders, the strength and efficiency of the police force, the methods of recording crimes, all these factors vary not only from time to time and from district to district, but differ also in respect of types of offender and particular forms of offence. The striking contrast between these difficulties and the high standard of accuracy required by present-day statistical research has given rise to an attitude of statistical nihilism which sometimes finds its expression in doubts about the value of official Criminal Statistics for criminological research. However, the apparent limits of statistical information do not justify discarding this source of evidence altogether. In a study of human behaviour and personal relationships, very few comprehensive statements can be verified. Our knowledge of man's actions and reactions always applies within certain specified limits only, and objectivity in the social sciences consists in the frank admission of those limits. With these qualifications, the present study relies on the figures of the official Criminal Statistics as its principal evidence and its obvious starting-point. Unless explicitly stated otherwise, all figures in the text and the tables of this study are taken from the annual volumes of *Criminal Statistics, England and Wales*, from privately circulated *Supplementary Statistics*, and from unprinted Home Office returns, or have been calculated from figures found in these materials. Rates computed from figures in the Criminal Statistics which apply to the country as a whole are referred to as national rates. Where conditions in individual districts are assessed they are mostly compared with figures which indicate average district rates. Owing to the different statistical basis, the two rates differ to a certain extent.

Throughout this survey the terms magistrates' courts and juvenile courts are used synonymously. In fact, a small number of juveniles are proceeded against in magistrates' courts which are not juvenile courts, because the young delinquents have been charged jointly with adult offenders. These cases amount to 5–6 per cent. of all juveniles appearing before the courts.

The small number of juvenile offenders found guilty by Quarter Sessions and Assizes is not included in the present report. For the years under observation, their average annual number was 576.

CHAPTER II

LOCAL VARIATIONS IN JUVENILE DELINQUENCY

Local Delinquency-rates

ANY investigation of the treatment practice of magistrates' courts in the 134 police districts of England and Wales must take into account the amount and structure of delinquency in different localities. Juvenile courts do not operate in a vacuum. Magistrates are likely to consider actual conditions as they prevail in their areas. They are influenced in their outlook by the rise and fall in the number of young offenders and the more serious or more trifling character of the offences they have to deal with. The first object of this study of the treatment practice of English juvenile courts was therefore a computation of local delinquency-rates for all 134 police districts. Such local delinquency-rates had to be calculated for the four statutory groups under the Children and Young Persons Act, 1933: boys of 8–13, girls of 8–13, boys of 14–17, and girls of 14–17.

The calculation of such local delinquency-rates met with considerable difficulties. There is no direct information available about the numbers of boys and girls of these age groups in each of the 134 police districts. Such specific local population figures had to be computed from ordinary sources of population statistics. Particular care had to be taken in the use of statistical sources, since the impact of the war and post-war conditions had affected contemporary population statistics. While young men were drafted into the forces and saw active service in different parts of the country and abroad, troops from other districts and American forces were stationed in many parts of England and Wales. The statistical publications of the Registrar-General fortunately give figures for administrative counties and county boroughs which, in general, coincide with the police districts. There are a number of exceptions to this rule. The Metropolitan Police District and Mid-Wales cover a wider area than one administrative county. Chester, Durham, and

Stafford as police districts include one or more county boroughs. Southampton includes the Isle of Wight. Adjustments had therefore to be made, by regrouping administrative areas in the Metropolitan Police District and elsewhere, so that the figures drawn from the census areas conform to the police districts in the Home Office returns.

For the calculation of population figures for the four relevant age groups and the two sexes in each police district the following sources were used.

1. *Estimates of the Sex and Age Distribution of the Civilian Population in Regions and Administrative Areas of England and Wales at 31 December 1947.*

This publication gives local figures for the two sexes and the following age groups: 0–4, 5–14, 15–17, 18–19, 20–24, and so on. The armed forces are entirely excluded, consequently the total figures in the adult age groups are not to be used if a true total population figure is required.

2. *Registrar-General's Statistical Review for 1949* (Part II).

This is an annual publication showing figures of total population for England and Wales as a whole. Figures are also provided for administrative areas. These local figures refer to the civilian population only. Sex and age groups are given as in the 1947 Estimates listed above.

3. *Registrar-General's Estimates of Total Population as at 30 June 1949.*

These figures are given for administrative areas but only for the age groups 0–15 and over. Sexes are not distinguished.

4. *Criminal Statistics for 1949.* Appendix II to the Introductory Note.

Estimated numbers are available in this publication for boys 8–13, 14–17, and girls 8–13 and 14–17. These figures refer to the country as a whole.

It seemed inadvisable to use the results of the 1951 Census for the purpose of this survey which deals with juvenile delinquency of the three years 1948, 1949, and 1950. The Preliminary Report of the 1951 Census does, however, emphasize a growing difference in the distribution of the sexes in various parts of the country. It would therefore be inaccurate to use the proportion of the numbers of boys and girls of the relevant age groups to the total population as it is given in the Criminal Statistics for the whole country, as a standard applicable to each district. The numbers given for persons of different age and sex groups in the Criminal Statistics are national estimates, apparently not based on an aggregate of local figures. The direct use of these estimated figures for the relevant local age groups would imply that the distribution of ages and sexes within the total population of each district is the same as within the country as a whole, an assumption refuted by any available evidence.

As a result of these considerations, a more complicated method of computing local age and sex groups as a basis for specific delinquency-rates had to be designed.[1] The starting-point was the total population 0–15 years in each district without differentiation into sexes, taken from the Registrar-General's Estimates as at 30 June 1949. This figure was converted into the number of males 5–14 years by using the relation between the various age and sex groups in the Estimates for 1947. Since figures for the lower age groups only are used, the outcome is not affected by the exclusion of the armed forces from the population figures in these Estimates. From the result, the number of males 5–14 years in each district, the required figure for males was calculated by applying the relation of the national estimate for boys in the Criminal Statistics to the 5–14 age group in the *Statistical Review* for the same year.[2]

By use of this method, the number of boys and girls of 8–13 years was calculated for each of the 134 police districts. The higher age group of 14–17 years was computed by accepting the relation between the two groups 8–13 years and 14–17 years for each sex according to the national estimates in the Criminal Statistics as a reliable standard for the corresponding relation in each district.

This calculation affords a reasonable degree of accuracy. It is not based on the assumption that the proportion of children

[1] The considerations in the text follow the advice generously given by Mr. T. S. Lodge.

[2] The formula used was as follows:

$$\frac{\text{M. and F. popn. for district}}{\text{ages 0–15. R.G. Est. 1949}} \times \frac{\text{5–14 (M.) 1947}}{\text{0–14 (M.+F.) 1947}} \times \frac{\text{8–13 (M.) C.S. 1949}}{\text{5–14 (M.) R.G. Rev. 1949}}$$

and young persons within the total population in each district corresponds to the same proportion within the national estimates of the Criminal Statistics. The projection of the distribution of ages and sexes from the national to the local level refers only to the proportion between certain younger age groups where considerable local differences are not probable. The increasing regional differences in the numerical relation between the sexes which have been confirmed by the *Preliminary Report to the 1951 Census* are apparently due to the migration of female workers in light industries and the presence of a large number of elderly women in southern health resorts. These facts do not affect the younger age groups. In spite of certain inevitable assumptions this method of calculation was, therefore, accepted as the best available. For each police district the numbers of the four relevant age and sex groups were computed. These specific local population figures appeared fairly adequate for the purpose of determining local delinquency-rates for boys and girls of 8–13 and of 14–17 per 1,000 persons of each sex and age group for three years in each district.

In all calculations and tabulations which follow the City of London has been omitted. The City is not a residential district. It has, according to the methods applied in this study, a juvenile population of no more than 206. Yet within the three years under review 138 juveniles were found guilty of indictable offences. It is most probable that the majority of these delinquents come from other areas outside the City boundaries, while only a few City dwellers fill the ranks of delinquents elsewhere. It would, therefore, be unrealistic to establish a delinquency rate for the City or to include such a rate in the calculations which follow.

Separate juvenile population figures could not be established for the three subdivisions of the Metropolitan Police District or for the separate police district in Tynemouth known as Tyne River Police. The Metropolitan Police District has, therefore, been taken as one, and Tyne River Police has been merged with Tynemouth.

The amount of juvenile delinquency, its rise and fall within certain periods, and its local variations cannot be determined without one further reservation. All observations in the discussion which follows are based on the figures for those found guilty by the courts. Obviously, they represent only part of the total number of actual law-breakers. However, the 'dark figure', that is the difference between the number of actual offenders and those who appear in the columns of criminal statistics, is always difficult to assess and appears particularly disturbing in the case of juvenile delinquents. Even variations in the actual crime-rate do not in themselves imply any moral judgement on the local population. Absconders from a nearby Approved School or Borstal who commit offences in the neighbourhood, troops recruited from other parts of the country, or young men employed in adjacent industrial centres may be responsible for unexpectedly high crime rates for certain age groups in particular districts. As long as the discussion is concerned only with youth before the courts, with the offenders with whom the magistrates are confronted, and with the various forms of treatment which they accord to them, the official Criminal Statistics and Home Office returns are a pertinent and accurate basis. However, it would be unrealistic to stop there and to evade the question of the social significance of those figures as symptoms of maladjustment and delinquency. For such a purpose a detailed analysis of the figures produced from official sources must be supplemented by any available evidence on social conditions, educational facilities, and the whole way of life in the community.

As a first step, the investigation has to envisage the extent of delinquency in the various age groups with which the courts in different parts of the country are confronted. Table IV shows delinquency-rates for 130 police districts both in respect of the four sex and age groups and for the total juvenile population. From these local delinquency-rates figures were obtained which represent the average rates for all police districts. The following figures show these averages in comparison with the corresponding national figures drawn from the official Criminal Statistics.

	Delinquency-rates for the period 1948–50 per 1,000 of the juvenile population				
	Boys 8–13	*Boys 14–17*	*Girls 8–13*	*Girls 14–17*	*Aggregate*
National figures . .	42·0	53·6	3·3	5·8	25·5
Average rates for all police districts	39·0	51·0	3·4	6·5	25·2

TABLE IV. *Local Delinquency-rates in England and Wales for the Three-year Period 1948–50*

Police district	Juvenile population	Delinquency-rate per 1,000 juveniles in each sex and age group: Boys 8–13	Boys 14–17	Girls 8–13	Girls 14–17	Delinquency rate for all juveniles 8–17
BEDFORDSHIRE	35,192	38·0	52·1	2·6	4·9	23·3
BERKSHIRE	33,417	23·6	48·7	2·1	3·7	17·5
Reading	13,171	23·9	48·3	3·7	8·9	18·8
BUCKINGHAMSHIRE	44,258	20·9	31·2	1·1	2·9	13·1
CAMBRIDGESHIRE	8,864	16·2	21·9	1·4	2·1	9·9
Cambridge	8,392	12·5	34·6	2·2	4·4	11·3
Isle of Ely	10,392	17·4	28·5	1·4	2·4	11·5
CHESHIRE	95,310	48·6	53·9	3·4	4·4	27·4
Birkenhead	17,763	104·4	91·2	9·7	10·5	55·6
Stockport	15,566	73·9	62·3	9·7	9·0	40·3
Wallasey	11,760	57·4	47·4	4·1	8·4	30·2
CORNWALL	36,372	24·6	37·8	3·2	6·7	16·8
CUMBERLAND	26,042	32·3	47·9	1·5	3·1	19·9
Carlisle	7,524	39·6	70·0	0·8	3·3	25·9
DERBYSHIRE	81,370	36·3	44·8	3·1	3·7	21·3
Derby	16,228	35·5	35·1	1·9	6·5	19·6
DEVONSHIRE	53,185	15·3	25·8	1·1	4·3	10·5
Exeter	8,387	61·9	70·0	5·0	11·1	36·5
Plymouth	23,415	30·5	47·0	1·7	5·0	19·5
DORSETSHIRE	31,980	41·8	46·0	3·3	7·2	24·2
DURHAM	133,680	63·0	69·0	4·2	6·4	35·3
Gateshead	14,678	60·5	82·4	4·1	8·1	36·8
S. Shields	13,357	56·8	58·9	1·4	3·3	30·2
Sunderland	24,105	43·8	57·6	4·4	6·4	27·1
ESSEX	91,080	24·1	36·5	1·7	4·2	15·8
Southend	16,045	47·0	49·4	7·5	13·2	28.9
GLOUCESTERSHIRE	59,465	24·4	37·1	1·2	3·5	15·4
Bristol	49,515	33·1	41·7	3·0	6·4	20·2
HEREFORDSHIRE	15,238	20·9	37·1	2·8	6·1	14·3
HERTFORDSHIRE	56,275	25·1	40·9	2·3	4·5	16·8
KENT	125,910	28·7	41·3	3·1	4·6	17·6
HUNTINGDONSHIRE	77,600	14·2	39·8	0·4	4·1	12·2
LANCASHIRE	234,640	31·5	48·0	2·1	3·3	19·9
Barrow-in-Furness	8,105	53·3	70·3	5·6	3·8	32·3
Blackburn	11,327	59·8	72·2	4·8	5·5	34·9
Blackpool	12,671	43·3	86·9	3·8	15·2	32·8
Bolton	17,934	26·5	35·8	1·7	3·1	16·1
Bootle	10,440	113·8	118·9	4·3	9·5	61·8
Burnley	8,630	48·7	44·9	7·7	6·5	27·7
Liverpool	108,050	99·8	105·7	4·8	11·7	55·0
Manchester	81,460	69·1	76·5	5·5	14·7	40·5
Oldham	12,975	68·6	64·7	6·3	4·8	37·1
Preston	13,720	39·4	54·7	4·6	4·1	24·7
Rochdale	8,840	76·5	64·3	9·0	6·3	40·7

TABLE IV. *Local Delinquency-rates in England and Wales for the Three-year Period 1948–50 (cont.)*

Police district	*Juvenile population*	*Delinquency-rate per 1,000 juveniles in each sex and age group*				*Delinquency rate for all juveniles 8–17*
		Boys 8–13	*Boys 14–17*	*Girls 8–13*	*Girls 14–17*	
St. Helens	13,165	55·4	79·0	1·5	9·7	36·6
Salford	21,432	56·2	59·1	1·7	4·6	30·8
Southport	7,772	26·3	46·7	4·3	2·4	18·7
Warrington	9,746	59·0	73·8	7·2	7·7	36·3
Wigan	10,108	67·5	57·5	1·8	1·8	33·6
LEICESTERSHIRE	41,370	27·6	38·6	2·8	3·3	17·3
Leicester	32,000	39·7	47·3	2·5	6·0	23·3
LINCOLNSHIRE (Holland)	12,580	35·8	43·3	1·2	5·9	20·7
,, (Kesteven)	14,580	33·6	36·9	2·3	5·1	19·2
,, (Lindsey)	36,532	37·3	38·9	3·6	4·9	21·2
Grimsby	13,192	116·2	97·5	6·1	11·6	55·0
Lincoln	7,489	43·6	36·3	5·8	7·5	24·0
Met. Police District	895,100	36·5	51·4	2·5	5·7	23·0
MONMOUTHSHIRE	39,890	56·0	64·5	3·9	4·9	32·0
Newport (Mon.)	12,695	78·4	65·7	3·8	6·4	40·0
NORFOLK	42,534	14·6	27·9	3·3	4·5	11·5
Norwich	13,517	35·2	46·5	4·7	9·7	22·8
Gt. Yarmouth	6,470	44·6	65·5	2·3	6·7	28·0
NORTHAMPTONSHIRE	29,376	32·1	34·4	3·6	2·9	18·3
Northampton	11,536	43·2	43·1	2·9	4·3	23·6
Peterborough	7,138	20·4	34·7	2·1	7·0	14·5
NORTHUMBERLAND	50,945	54·5	59·9	3·9	4·6	30·6
Newcastle upon Tyne	34,825	53·7	72·5	1·7	7·5	32·1
Tynemouth	8,307	81·6	89·6	3·3	2·9	44·3
NOTTINGHAMSHIRE	63,425	37·9	42·5	2·9	3·0	21·5
Nottingham	36,340	33·9	47·6	3·6	9·1	22·1
OXFORDSHIRE	20,000	24·8	42·1	1·1	3·4	16·3
Oxford	10,933	27·2	51·0	3·0	5·7	19·7
RUTLANDSHIRE	2,556	14·9	23·7	1·2	7·0	10·6
SHROPSHIRE	34,138	24·6	41·5	2·9	4·0	16·9
SOMERSETSHIRE	53,130	22·8	42·7	1·3	3·4	15·9
Bath	8,536	34·5	48·6	3·9	2·2	19·0
SOUTHAMPTON	82,470	37·0	43·3	3·0	4·9	21·6
Bournemouth	13,128	23·6	44·7	3·5	7·6	17·9
Portsmouth	27,110	38·7	41·0	4·1	8·3	22·7
Southampton	22,047	53·0	53·1	4·7	11·0	30·3
STAFFORDSHIRE	131,380	39·0	44·0	3·9	3·9	22·1
Stoke-on-Trent	34,277	39·7	45·2	5·9	7·8	24·4
Walsall	14,888	48·8	51·7	7·7	6·7	28·8
Wolverhampton	19,698	51·1	59·7	5·1	6·6	30·1
SUFFOLK E.	25,820	27·1	44·5	2·7	5·8	18·6
Ipswich	12,290	44·5	59·6	4·2	7·6	27·6
SUFFOLK W.	12,902	17·9	31·9	1·6	2·9	12·4

TABLE IV. *Local Delinquency-rates in England and Wales for the Three-year Period 1948–50 (cont.)*

Police district	Juvenile population	Delinquency-rate per 1,000 juveniles in each sex and age group: Boys 8–13	Boys 14–17	Girls 8–13	Girls 14–17	Delinquency rate for all juveniles 8–17
SURREY	89,590	19·3	29·8	1·8	3·1	12·4
SUSSEX E.	35,530	18·4	30·2	1·3	4·3	12·5
Brighton	16,460	28·4	36·3	2·4	4·2	17·1
Eastbourne	5,790	25·2	32·5	2·1	3·2	15·1
Hastings	6,786	37·4	45·5	6·7	7·3	23·7
SUSSEX W.	34,930	33·8	51·0	2·9	6·9	22·1
WARWICKSHIRE	57,660	26·5	47·3	1·8	4·1	18·1
Birmingham	135,920	64·4	53·7	5·8	9·4	33·8
Coventry	31,070	43·3	56·1	5·6	8·4	27·3
WESTMORLAND	7,540	12·8	33·7	1·2	—	10·3
WILTSHIRE	41,950	27·0	35·2	1·9	6·4	16·7
WORCESTERSHIRE	47,500	36·1	42·1	3·2	5·4	21·2
Dudley	7,948	49·6	58·7	7·2	8·6	30·5
Worcester	7,196	39·4	46·3	1·7	4·3	22·3
YORKSHIRE E.	24,020	31·7	54·5	2·8	3·6	21·4
Hull	41,640	68·8	72·9	4·9	7·4	38·4
YORKSHIRE N.	43,460	48·3	62·2	3·1	4·7	28·5
Middlesbrough	19,833	99·0	85·1	12·8	21·0	55·6
York	12,073	26·1	38·9	4·1	6·4	17·8
YORKSHIRE W.	188,550	70·0	70·5	4·8	4·9	38·1
Barnsley	9,646	48·5	69·7	2·9	9·7	30·6
Bradford	31,210	45·8	50·0	4·1	5·8	26·2
Dewsbury	6,203	50·0	62·5	1·0	3·0	27·6
Doncaster	9,886	52·5	72·8	1·8	8·8	31·9
Halifax	10,424	36·4	59·9	8·1	6·5	26·0
Huddersfield	13,092	41·0	49·9	6·0	3·3	24·8
Leeds	56,840	55·6	61·2	5·5	9·7	32·6
Rotherham	10,563	52·7	57·2	8·0	7·6	31·3
Sheffield	59,503	28·9	36·2	2·4	5·9	17·6
Wakefield	7,040	27·5	39·5	1·3	5·9	17·2
ANGLESEY	5,774	15·6	30·4	0·5	2·1	10·9
CAERNARVONSHIRE	13,319	34·0	28·6	3·2	3·7	18·0
CARDIGANSHIRE	5,471	17·6	28·2	3·3	3·4	12·2
CARMARTHENSHIRE	18,615	32·9	27·4	2·6	4·6	17·3
DENBIGHSHIRE	19,832	33·0	48·8	2·1	6·2	21·1
FLINTSHIRE	16,750	27·7	33·2	3·4	4·4	16·9
GLAMORGANSHIRE	88,940	59·0	65·5	3·7	5·2	33·1
Cardiff	28,390	50·6	67·5	4·5	7·9	31·3
Merthyr Tydvil	7,159	50·6	47·4	2·5	8·7	27·4
Swansea	18,996	72·0	67·3	3·4	5·7	36·9
MERIONETHSHIRE	4,344	13·4	37·5	0·7	—	11·1
MID-WALES	22,210	15·2	28·9	0·8	5·9	10·3
PEMBROKESHIRE	10,466	16·2	23·7	1·4	5·9	10·9

High-delinquency and Low-delinquency Areas

It is essential for a survey of juvenile delinquency and the treatment practice of the courts to locate those districts which are characterized by unusually high or exceptionally low delinquency-rates. In Table V thirteen areas have been listed as high-delinquency areas, and in Table VI seventeen districts as low-delinquency areas. The assignment of districts to the groups of either high-delinquency or low-delinquency areas has been based on the delinquency-rates for all juveniles of both sexes between 8 and 17 years as they are given in the last column of Tables V and VI. In this context the limits were determined by the district average of 25·2 plus or minus the standard deviation of 11·5, with the resulting figures rounded up and down to 37 on the high and 13 on the low side of the scale.

TABLE V. *Areas of High Delinquency-rates for All Juveniles 8–17 for the Period 1948–50*

District	*Delinquency-rate per 1,000 juveniles in each age and sex group*				*Delinquency-rate for all juveniles*
	Boys 8–13	*Boys 14–17*	*Girls 8–13*	*Girls 14–17*	*8–17*
Bootle	113·8	118·9	4·3	9·5	61·8
Middlesbrough	99·0	85·1	12·8	21·0	55·6
Birkenhead	104·4	91·2	9·7	10·5	55·6
Liverpool	99·8	105·7	4·8	11·7	55·0
Grimsby	116·2	97·5	6·1	11·6	55·0
Tynemouth	81·6	89·6	3·3	2·9	44·3
Rochdale	76·5	64·3	9·0	6·3	40·7
Manchester	69·1	76·5	5·5	14·7	40·5
Stockport	73·9	62·3	9·7	9·0	40·3
Newport (Mon.)	78·4	65·7	3·8	6·4	40·0
Hull	68·8	72·9	4·9	7·4	38·4
YORKSHIRE W.	70·0	70·5	4·8	4·9	38·1
Oldham	68·6	64·7	6·3	4·8	37·1

While these tabulations are based on the statutory age groups of children and young persons in the meaning of section 107(1) of the Children and Young Persons Act, 1933, there are, from a criminological point of view, considerable differences within each group. According to the *Criminal Statistics for 1950*, where national delinquency-rates are given for each yearly age group between 8 and 20 years, between 1938 and 1950 the peak age in the delinquency of boys has shifted from 13 to 14 years. The delinquency in the two last years (12 and 13) in the children's group comes very near to the record figure for boys of 14 and is only balanced by the very small rates for boys of 8 and 9. The statutory dividing line at the fourteenth birthday no longer indicates the significant distinction between school-children and wage-earners, although all children under 14 must go to

TABLE VI. *Areas of Low Delinquency-rates for All Juveniles 8–17 for the Period 1948–50*

District	*Delinquency-rate per 1,000 juveniles in each age and sex group*				*Delinquency-rate for all juveniles 8–17*
	Boys 8–13	*Boys 14–17*	*Girls 8–13*	*Girls 14–17*	
CAMBRIDGESHIRE	16·2	21·9	1·4	2·1	9·9
WESTMORLAND	12·8	33·7	1·2	—	10·3
MID-WALES	15·2	28·9	0·8	5·9	10·3
DEVONSHIRE	15·3	25·8	1·1	4·3	10·5
RUTLANDSHIRE	14·7	23·7	1·3	7·0	10·6
ANGLESEY	15·6	30·4	0·5	2·1	10·9
PEMBROKESHIRE	16·2	23·7	1·4	5·9	10·9
MERIONETHSHIRE	13·4	37·5	0·7	—	11·1
Cambridge	12·5	34·6	2·2	4·4	11·3
Isle of Ely	17·4	28·5	1·4	2·4	11·5
NORFOLK	14·6	27·9	3·3	4·5	11·5
HUNTINGDONSHIRE	14·2	39·8	0·4	4·1	12·2
CARDIGANSHIRE	17·6	28·2	3·3	3·4	12·2
SUFFOLK W.	17·9	31·9	1·6	2·9	12·4
SURREY	19·3	29·8	1·8	3.1	12·4
SUSSEX E.	18·4	30·2	1·3	4·3	12·5
BUCKINGHAMSHIRE	20·9	31·2	1·1	2·9	13·1

school and most, but not all, of the young persons are in paid employment. In the three years under discussion, young persons of 14 and under 15 years still had to attend school. The respective contribution to juvenile delinquency of either school-children or young wage-earners can therefore only be established by an analysis of representative case studies. Nevertheless, the study of the local delinquency-rates for the two statutory age groups reveals a characteristic difference. For boys of the age group 14–17 the number of conspicuously high- or low-delinquency areas is surprisingly small, while for junior boys of

8–13 years the exceptionally high or low delinquency-rates are spread over a wider number of districts. This observation suggests that local differences in the amount of juvenile delinquency are very much due to variations in the delinquency of boys of tender years. For junior boys these striking differences are probably affected by variations in the 'dark figure'. For them, more than for older delinquents, outstanding differences in court figures represent not only frequent and infrequent criminal activities but also readiness or reluctance on the part of the public or the police to bring the young law-breaker before the court.

The geographical distribution of high-delinquency and low-delinquency areas in the post-war period is shown at the lower side of Map 1. Among the thirteen high-delinquency areas are eight ports, mostly in the north of England, and Manchester, Rochdale, Stockport, Oldham, and the West Riding of Yorkshire. There are seventeen low-delinquency areas of which sixteen are rural areas; six, including Surrey and Devonshire, in the south, four as a rather coherent group in the mid-East, five in Wales, and one in the North. The thirteen high-delinquency areas cover a juvenile population of 539,471 out of a total juvenile population in England and Wales of more than five million, while the seventeen low-delinquency areas have a juvenile population of 370,798.

It may appear a surprising result of these calculations that in the assessment of high-delinquency areas no reference has been made to juvenile delinquency in London. However, a study of general conviction rates confirms the impression that there is nothing unusual with regard to the crime situation in the Metropolis as far as it is reflected in court appearances. In the Metropolitan Police District and the City of London the rate of persons found guilty of indictable offences at magistrates' courts per 10,000 of population was 17 for 1938 and 25 for 1952. These figures correspond exactly both for the years before and after the war with the national figures for the whole country. For an interpretation of this conformity it has to be remembered that, both before and after the war, the jurisdiction of the Metropolitan Police District covered approximately one-fifth of the total population of England and Wales. There are, however, reasons to suggest that the difference in the actual amount of

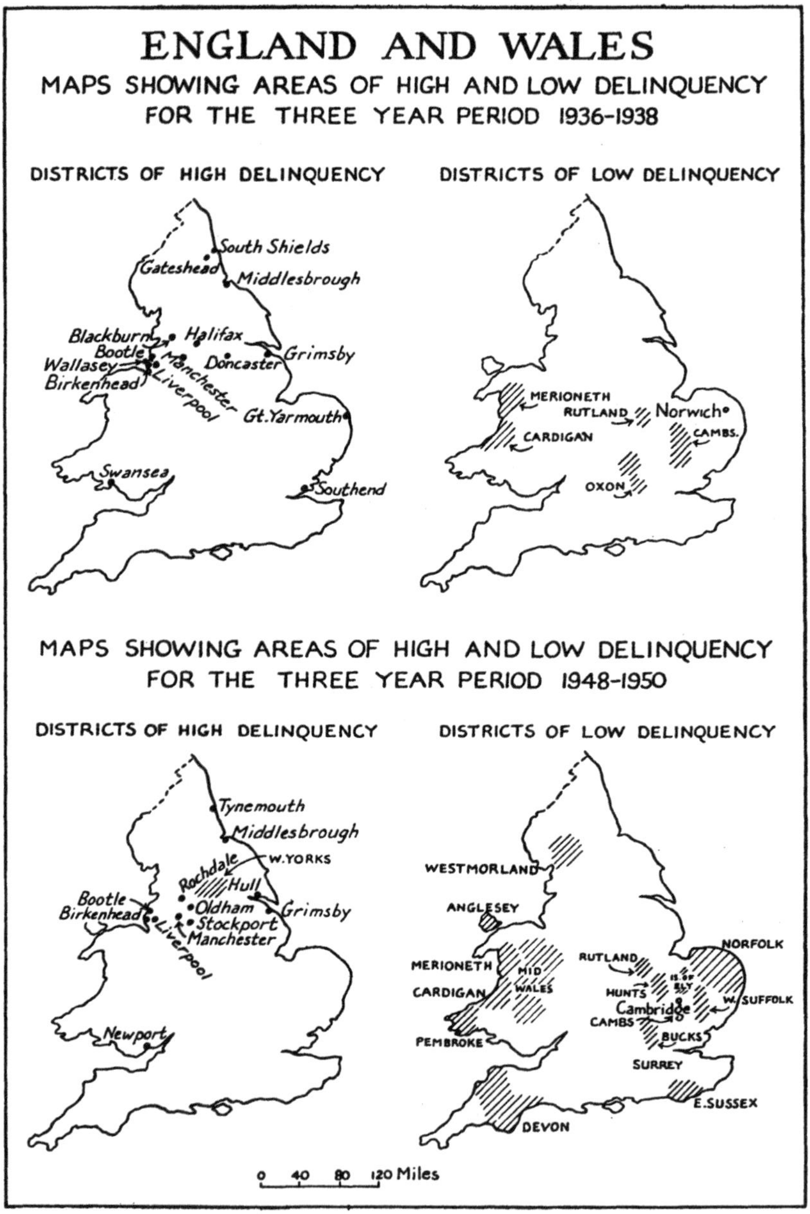
ENGLAND AND WALES
MAPS SHOWING AREAS OF HIGH AND LOW DELINQUENCY
FOR THE THREE YEAR PERIOD 1936-1938
DISTRICTS OF HIGH DELINQUENCY
South Shields
Gateshead
Middlesbrough
Blackburn
Halifax
Bootle
Wallasey
Birkenhead
Manchester
Liverpool
Doncaster
Grimsby
Gt. Yarmouth
Swansea
Southend
DISTRICTS OF LOW DELINQUENCY
MERIONETH
RUTLAND
Norwich
CARDIGAN
CAMBS.
OXON
MAPS SHOWING AREAS OF HIGH AND LOW DELINQUENCY
FOR THE THREE YEAR PERIOD 1948-1950
DISTRICTS OF HIGH DELINQUENCY
Tynemouth
Middlesbrough
Rochdale
W. YORKS
Hull
Bootle
Birkenhead
Oldham
Stockport
Manchester
Grimsby
Liverpool
Newport
DISTRICTS OF LOW DELINQUENCY
WESTMORLAND
ANGLESEY
NORFOLK
MERIONETH
MID WALES
RUTLAND
CARDIGAN
HUNTS
Cambridge
W. SUFFOLK
CAMBS
BUCKS
PEMBROKE
SURREY
E. SUSSEX
DEVON
0 40 80 120 Miles

Map 1

crime between the Metropolis and the country as a whole is greater than the conviction-rates indicate. The percentage of reported crime cleared up by the Metropolitan Police fell from the pre-war level of 27·1 to 25·1 in 1946 and rose beyond the pre-war standard to 31·9 in 1952, while the police forces in the rest of the country claimed detection-rates of 61 in 1938, of 47 in 1948, and of 51 in 1952. These lower detection-rates in the Metropolis mean that behind the normal rates of persons found guilty there is actually a higher incidence of crime. In 1952 the rate of crimes known to the police per 10,000 of total population in the Metropolitan Police District and the City of London was 13·3 and thus exceeded the corresponding figure for the rest of the country which was 11·3 in the same year.[1] For an assessment of juvenile delinquency, it must be remembered that there are six juvenile courts in London. Their venue covers districts widely differing in social structure and the circumstances in which children are brought up. One has therefore to expect certain variations in the amount and forms of juvenile delinquency in London. These observations make it desirable to undertake an investigation into the specific problems of delinquency and court practice in the Capital. In the meantime, within the wider context of the present study of conditions in the whole country, the data from the Metropolis must be seen in the right proportion. On the whole, the evidence does not justify the singling out of the Metropolitan Police District for the study of selected areas with exceptional features of juvenile delinquency.

The thirteen high-delinquency areas include only one county police district, the West Riding of Yorkshire, which is interspersed with industrial boroughs. All but one of the seventeen low-delinquency areas are rural counties. It seemed therefore advisable to calculate separate mean figures for industrial and rural districts. Since many, if not most, of the administrative counties of England and Wales are of a more or less mixed industrial and rural character, any attempt to divide the country into an industrial and a rural part would be misleading. Instead the twenty-one police districts of Lancashire and

[1] Figures calculated from the data extracted from *Reports of the Commissioner of Police for the Metropolis*, *Criminal Statistics*, and statistical material provided by the Home Office.

Staffordshire with a total juvenile population of 792,358 were chosen to represent the industrial community. These districts were Lancashire, Barrow, Blackburn, Blackpool, Bolton, Bootle, Burnley, Liverpool, Manchester, Oldham, Preston, Rochdale, St. Helens, Salford, Southport, Warrington, Wigan, Staffordshire, Stoke-on-Trent, Walsall, and Wolverhampton. Likewise, seven counties with a predominantly rural character and a total juvenile population of 151,488 were selected to illustrate the pattern of delinquency in the countryside, Sussex, Cornwall, Rutland, Huntingdonshire, Cambridgeshire, Isle of Ely, and Herefordshire. From the local delinquency-rates given in Table IV mean delinquency rates were calculated for the four sex and age groups both in the industrial and in the rural districts. The result is shown in the following three rows of figures, where the industrial and rural means are compared with the total average district rate.

	Boys 8–13	*Boys 14–17*	*Girls 8–13*	*Girls 14–17*	*Aggregate 8–17*
Industrial mean	55·9	64·7	4·7	6·5	32·3
Rural mean	19·2	32·8	1·8	4·9	13·2
Mean for all districts in England and Wales	39·0	51·0	3·4	6·5	25·2

Again the outstanding difference in the delinquency of industrial and rural areas is to be found in boys of 8–13 years.

It is fair to assume that life in the country offers more and better opportunities for harmless youthful activities than the densely populated quarters of industrial towns. At the same time it is possible that there is less opportunity and less inclination in the country to bring small boys before a court of justice. For the purpose of the present study the calculations of industrial and rural means provide certain standards for the assessment of delinquency in individual districts. By comparison with the industrial and rural means, local delinquency rates in specified places will be seen in proper proportion.

The classification of high- and low-delinquency areas still contains a certain generalization. A district may be a high-delinquency area either because numerous juveniles from all age groups between 8 and 17 years have to appear before the court, or because one particular age group of boys or girls has an exceedingly high rate of delinquency. For an adequate description of the crime situation in a high-delinquency and

TABLE VII. *Areas with High and Low Delinquency-rates in more than One Sex and Age Group*

District	*Delinquency-rate per 1,000 juveniles in each sex and age group*				*Delinquency-rate for all juveniles 8–17*
	Boys 8–13	*Boys 14–17*	*Girls 8–13*	*Girls 14–17*	
HIGH-DELINQUENCY AREAS					
Consistency in 4 groups					
Middlesbrough	99·0	85·1	12·8	21·0	55·6
Birkenhead	104·4	91·2	9·7	10·5	55·6
Consistency in 3 groups					
Liverpool	99·8	105·7	4·8	11·7	55·0
Grimsby	116·2	97·5	6·1	11·6	55·0
Consistency in 2 groups					
Bootle	113·8	118·9	4·3	9·5	61·8
Tynemouth	81·6	89·6	3·3	2·9	44·3
LOW-DELINQUENCY AREAS					
Consistency in 4 groups					
ANGLESEY	15·6	30·4	0·5	2·1	10·9
Consistency in 3 groups					
CAMBRIDGESHIRE	16·2	21·9	1·4	2·1	9·9
WESTMORLAND	12·8	33·7	1·2	—	10·3
MID-WALES	15·2	28·9	0·8	5·9	10·3
DEVONSHIRE	15·3	25·8	1·1	4·3	10·3
MERIONETHSHIRE	13·4	37·5	0·7	—	11·1
Consistency in 2 groups					
RUTLANDSHIRE	14·7	23·7	1·3	7·0	10·6
PEMBROKESHIRE	16·2	23·7	1·4	5·9	10·9
Isle of Ely	17·4	28·5	1·4	2·4	11·5
NORFOLK	14·6	27·9	3·3	4·5	11·5
HUNTINGDONSHIRE	14·2	39·8	0·4	4·1	12·2

High delinquency-rates were taken to be those over the mean $+1{\cdot}5\times$ the standard deviation for each sex and age group, i.e. boys 8–13, 76; boys 14–17, 79·5; girls 8–13, 6·7; girls 14–17, 10·2. Limits beyond which rates were considered to be low were: boys 8–13, 17; boys 14–17, 32; girls 8–13, 1·2; girls 14–17, 2·8.

a low-delinquency area, due consideration must be given to the internal structure of the high and low amount of juvenile delinquency. Tables V and VI show not only the aggregate delinquency-rates for all juveniles, but also specific crime-rates for each of the four sex and age groups. The evidence suggests that there is a certain amount of consistency in the sense that there are places which are outstanding in their high or low delinquency-rates in more than one of the four subgroups of juvenile offenders. These districts are listed in Table VII. Middlesbrough and Birkenhead, which rank very high on the list of high-delinquency areas, have high delinquency-rates throughout all four

TABLE VIII. *Delinquency-rates for Certain Specified Parts of England and Wales, 1948–50*

Area	Juvenile population	Delinquency-rate per 1,000 juveniles in each sex and age group				Delinquency-rate for all juveniles 8–17
		Boys 8–13	Boys 14–17	Girls 8–13	Girls 14–17	
M.P.D.	895,100	36·5	51·4	2·5	5·7	23·0
Northern Counties	1,376,625	57·0	66·7	3·6	6·5	32·9
Wales						
Industrial	142,985	59·3	61·9	3·5	6·9	30·7
Rural	116,781	22·8	31·8	2·2	4·0	14·3
Average for all Wales	259,766	34·0	41·1	2·6	4·9	23·3
East Anglia						
Urban	19,987	39·9	56·0	3·5	8·2	25·4
Rural	77,982	15·0	28·5	1·7	3·6	11·3
Average for whole of East Anglia	97,969	22·1	37·5	2·4	4·8	15·3

groups of juveniles. Bootle heads the list of high-delinquency areas on account of the exceedingly high rate of 118·9 for boys of 14–17 years. This is an exceptionally high rate for senior boys, far above the mean for senior boys in industrial places, which amounts to 64·7.

While the investigation so far has been focused on rates of delinquency in individual police districts, it is also desirable to know something about the amount and structure of juvenile delinquency within certain wider regions. It would, however, be of little use to calculate regional delinquency-rates for the customary geographical subdivisions of the country. Most of these areas, like the North, the Midlands, and the South, comprise great varieties in social structure and economic conditions. Crime-rates of different geographical units are not comparable unless either they have a similar social structure, so that a comparison of their respective criminality allows certain conclusions about the inhabitants' character and mode of life, or they have distinct social characteristics of their own so that a comparison throws some light on the criminological significance of the social factors involved. For this reason only a few regions were selected which are fairly homogeneous in their social and economic character. They are a group of four northern industrial counties, Lancashire, Yorkshire, Northumberland, and Durham; the Metropolitan Police District; industrial and rural Wales; and urban and rural East Anglia. Table VIII shows the most intense delinquency in the northern counties and industrial Wales, and a notably small delinquency-rate in the rural parts of East Anglia. Again, in the two industrial areas in the north and in Wales, the delinquency-rates of junior boys are high in comparison with rural places, and thus come near to the rate for senior boys. On the whole, the low delinquency-rates for girls show less variation than the formidable rates for boys.

Pre-war and Post-war Delinquency

The picture of juvenile delinquency in England and Wales would be incomplete without a comparison with past experience. The present criminal situation must be interpreted in the light of the rise and fall of crime in the course of the years. English Criminal Statistics before 1939 contained for each district the number of juveniles, without discrimination as to age and sex, found guilty of indictable offences, with the treatment awarded to them. In order to make a reliable comparison feasible, allowance had to be made for the changes in the boundaries of administrative areas which had taken place in the meantime. Therefore, the pre-war data have been adjusted so that they are comparable with the figures for 1948–50. For the presentation of delinquency-rates for 1936–8 in districts corresponding to the police districts of 1948–50, the total of juvenile population was calculated on the assumption that the proportion between the juvenile population and the total population in each district corresponds to the proportion between juvenile and total population which the Criminal Statistics give for the whole country. This somewhat crude method had been rejected when specific population figures and delinquency-rates were calculated for the four sex and age groups for 1948–50. Since, for 1936–8, only aggregate figures for juveniles are available, there was no alternative but to accept in each district a proportion of 0·143 of the total population as the number of juveniles.

A considerable increase in juvenile delinquency in England and Wales has been widely accepted as an established fact and seems to be confirmed by common experience. According to Criminal Statistics, in the three-year pre-war period 1936–8 out of 1,000 juveniles 14·3 were found guilty of indictable offences; in the three post-war years 1948–50 the rate was 25·5. Within the same period the much smaller number of juveniles in need of care and protection, including those beyond control and truants, rose from 6,355 for the three-year span 1936–8 to 13,737 for the three years 1948–50. This means an increase from 0·61 per 1,000 of all persons under 17 years of age to 1·3. This is an increase of 0·69 per 1,000, or a rise of 113 per cent. over the pre-war figure.

There are three reasons which justify the assumption that the rise in the number of juveniles found guilty by the courts is not only due to more frequent prosecutions, but represents, at least to a certain extent, an actual increase in the number of juveniles who committed offences. All European countries, however much they may differ in their reaction to juvenile delinquency and in the frequency and methods of prosecution, had characteristic war and post-war peaks in juvenile delinquency, while in the actual timing of the ups and downs of the delinquency curve and in the point at which it begins to flatten out, individual countries show considerable differences. Secondly, the increase in the number of convictions has not been limited to juvenile offenders alone, but appears in other age groups as well where a changing attitude in reporting cases to the police and in prosecuting offenders is less probable. Finally, the increase in the number of juveniles found guilty coincided with a temporary decrease in the proportion of suspected offences cleared up by the police. Before the war, in the whole country, every second indictable offence known to the police was cleared up. This proportion went down to 43 per cent. in 1948 and then climbed up again to 47 in 1949. As these somewhat smaller percentages of cases cleared up resulted in a considerably higher number of prosecutions and convictions, the police must have been concerned with a markedly higher number of crimes. This is indicated, for the period under observation, by a steep rise in the number of crimes known to the police. The high detection-rate of the year 1938 resulted in a total of 141,854 cases cleared up, but the comparatively low detection-rate of the year 1948 in 225,638 cases cleared up, which suggests that the fluctuations in detection-rates alone ought not to be interpreted as symptoms of decreasing standards in police efficiency. At the same time, it would not be right to explain these figures solely as the result of greater vigilance on the part of the police and a growing anxiety on the part of the public, and not also as an increase in the actual number of crimes committed. On the strength of these observations the hypothesis of an actual rise in juvenile delinquency seems justified.

The rise in crime from the pre-war to the post-war level was much more characteristic of juveniles than of the higher age-groups. While, according to Criminal Statistics, from 1936–8 to 1948–50 the delinquency-rates for juveniles of 8 and under 17 years increased from 14·3 to 25·5, the crime-rates for adolescents of 17 and under 21 years rose from 12·6 to 17·4 and the crime-rates of adults of 21 and over from 4·0 to 6·3. This means for juveniles a percentage rise of 78, for adolescents of 38, and for adults of 54.

For an interpretation of these figures one has to consider simultaneously the two factors which determine the increased amount of post-war crime, the level attained before the outbreak of the war, and the pace of the recent rise in convictions. The moderate crime-rate of adults increased by more than half its pre-war standard, the adolescent crime-rate which was more significant, though still not very high, rose by more than a third, but the high crime-rate of juveniles by more than three-quarters. It is thus unfortunate that the juveniles, as the group with the highest crime-rate before the war, had at the same time the steepest rise in delinquency-rates. However, the group of adults, comprising all persons of 21 years and over, includes subgroups of widely differing criminality. Young men between 21 and 30, though with a much lower incidence of crime than juveniles, had the same steep rise in their crime-rate which rose by nearly 75 per cent. from 1·4 to 2·3 per 1,000 for three years.

The striking rise in juvenile delinquency from high pre-war crime-rates to even more spectacular post-war figures is largely a reflection of the crime situation in big industrial towns. The most characteristic difference in the criminality of industrial places and rural districts applies to juveniles. Both before and after the war industrial places with their large numbers of juvenile delinquents had a higher delinquency-rate than the country as a whole, while the rural districts with their smaller numbers of young law-breakers remained below the national mean delinquency-rate. Within this pattern, however, the moderate rural delinquency-rate doubled and thus even slightly exceeded the percentual increase in the high industrial delinquency-rates. This seems to indicate that whatever factors are deemed to be responsible for post-war delinquency, they have been at work in town and country alike. In the numerical contribution to the rising tide of post-war delinquency in the country as a whole, the most significant share falls upon big industrial places. This becomes even more evident in the light of recent population trends. The process of the ageing of the population is more notable in industrial than in rural parts of the country. The high rates of juvenile delinquency refer to places where the fall in the total number of juvenile population is more conspicuous than in rural districts, and yet in rural districts juveniles appear less frequently before the courts. Between 1937 and 1949 the number of juveniles in selected industrial places decreased by 15·1 per cent. and in rural districts only by 12·6 per cent. Subject to further corroborating evidence, these observations seem to suggest that the high rates of juvenile delinquency in big industrial places cannot be attributed to masses of newcomers attracted by and ill-absorbed in the maelstrom of growing urbanization. A study of adolescent crime throws further light on this problem. While the rural juvenile delinquency-rate, after a steep rise, still remains markedly below the industrial mean, the crime-rate of adolescents in rural districts rose from 8·9 to 13·2 and thus slightly exceeds the corresponding rate in industrial places which is 12·8. The relative preponderance of adolescent criminality in rural areas has a certain parallel in the population movement. There was a slight increase in the total number of adolescents in rural districts while in selected industrial places their number fell by 15·2 per cent., almost the same rate as the rate of decrease in the number of juveniles. In these localities population trends are thus the same for adolescents and juveniles, and yet the increase in juvenile delinquency markedly surpasses the rise in adolescent

TABLE IX. *Areas Showing High Rates of Juvenile Delinquency in the Periods 1936–8 and 1948–50*

1936–8		*1948–50*	
District	*Rate*	*District*	*Rate*
Middlesbrough .	48·2	Bootle . . .	61·8
Liverpool . .	43·6	Middlesbrough. .	55·6
Bootle . . .	31·6	Birkenhead . .	55·6
Gateshead . .	30·2	Liverpool . .	55·0
S. Shields . .	26·2	Grimsby . . .	55·0
Birkenhead . .	24·8	Tynemouth . .	44·3
Halifax . . .	23·8	Rochdale . .	40·7
Wallasey . .	23·2	Manchester . .	40·5
Manchester . .	23·1	Stockport . .	40·3
Grimsby . .	23·0	Newport (Mon.) .	40·0
Swansea . .	22·7	Hull . . .	38·4
Southend . .	22·2	YORKSHIRE W. . .	38·1
Gt. Yarmouth .	22·2	Oldham . . .	37·1
Blackburn . .	22·0		
Doncaster . .	21·8		

crime. This observation confirms the impression that juvenile delinquency, more than other forms of criminality, is conspicuous in big industrial places.

The preceding figures illustrate the trend of crime and delinquency from pre-war years to the post-war period for the country as a whole with certain reference to characteristic differences between industrial and rural districts. Once more the question arises how the general trend in juvenile delinquency is reflected in the light of local experience. The rise and fall in juvenile delinquency must therefore be followed up in individual police districts within the various parts of England and Wales. Tables IX and X and Map 1 show, for juvenile delinquents in general, those districts which were high- and low-delinquency areas before and after the war. If one compares the spread of high- and low-delinquency areas in 1936–8 with the more recent conditions in 1948–50, the impression prevails that there has been a relative consistency with regard to those areas which have the most intense delinquency, and a certain shifting of the weight of crime to other places where delinquency is more moderate. All five districts which in the triennium 1948–50 were outstanding in crime, areas with a delinquency-rate of 55

TABLE X. *Areas Showing Low Rates of Juvenile Delinquency in the Periods 1936–8 and 1948–50*

1936–8		*1948–50*	
District	*Rate*	*District*	*Rate*
RUTLANDSHIRE	1·6	CAMBRIDGESHIRE	9·9
CAMBRIDGESHIRE	2·6	WESTMORLAND	10·3
Norwich	3·5	MID-WALES	10·3
OXFORDSHIRE	3·6	DEVONSHIRE	10·5
CARDIGANSHIRE	4·7	RUTLANDSHIRE	10·6
MERIONETHSHIRE	4·8	ANGLESEY	10·9
		PEMBROKESHIRE	10·9
		MERIONETHSHIRE	11·1
		Cambridge	11·3
		Isle of Ely	11·5
		NORFOLK	11·5
		HUNTINGDONSHIRE	12·2
		CARDIGANSHIRE	12·2
		SUSSEX E.	12·5
		SUFFOLK W.	12·4
		SURREY	12·4
		BUCKINGHAMSHIRE	13·1

and more per 1,000 juveniles, Bootle, Middlesbrough, Birkenhead, Liverpool, and Grimsby, were also high-delinquency areas before the war. Manchester, too, appears as a high-delinquency area then and now. Nine districts have ceased to rank as high-delinquency areas and their place has been taken by seven other districts. Four other counties from the six pre-war low-delinquency areas, Cambridgeshire, Rutland, Cardigan, and Merioneth, have maintained their place on the low-delinquency list after the war.

For the interpretation of these statistical results it must be kept in mind that consistency and inconsistency with regard to high and low delinquency-rates refer to a time with a rising trend in juvenile delinquency in general. All districts, even those which succeeded in remaining at the bottom of the scale, show markedly increased figures as compared with pre-war standards. However, the tempo and the pace of the general rise in the rates of juvenile delinquency are not everywhere the same. In Table XI twenty districts are listed where the increase in local delinquency-rates greatly exceeded the average increase for all districts. It is in the industrial towns, in Monmouth and

TABLE XI. *Areas Showing Considerable Deviation from the Mean Difference between the Delinquency-rates for 1936–8 and 1948–50*

District	*Rate 1936–8*	*Rate 1948–50*	*Difference*	*Percentage increase*
Grimsby	23·0	55·0	32·0	139
Tynemouth	13·1	44·3	31·2	238
Birkenhead	24·8	55·6	30·8	125
Bootle	31·6	61·8	30·2	95
Rochdale	13·4	40·7	27·3	203
Oldham	10·0	37·1	27·1	271
Stockport	13·8	40·3	26·5	199
Warrington	12·9	36·3	23·4	181
YORKSHIRE W.	15·4	38·1	22·7	147
Exeter	14·2	36·5	22·3	150
Newport (Mon.)	20·6	40·0	19·4	94
Rotherham	12·0	31·3	19·3	160
St. Helens	17·7	36·6	18·9	106
MONMOUTHSHIRE	13·9	32·0	18·1	130
Hull	20·7	38·4	17·7	85
Blackpool	15·3	32·8	17·5	114
Manchester	23·1	40·5	17·4	75
Newcastle	14·7	32·1	17·4	117
Norwich	3·5	22·8	19·3	551
Leeds	16·0	32·5	16·5	103

the West Riding of Yorkshire, where the upward tendency is most conspicuous. A steep rise in crime-rates alone does not determine the contribution which a particular place has made to the extensive post-war criminality. The true significance of any local rise in crime-rates depends, apart from the size of the locality, on the high or low level of delinquency from which the upward movement started. The high rates of the country's juvenile delinquency during and after the war are the result of an even and moderately steep rise in high-delinquency areas as well as of an exceedingly steep rise in medium- and low-delinquency areas. Among the first seven towns on the list which show an increase in their delinquency-rate of more than twice the average for all districts, there are three pre-war high-delinquency areas, Grimsby, Birkenhead, and Bootle, with a moderate rise between 95 and 139 per cent. of their already inflated pre-war delinquency. The four other places, Tynemouth, Rochdale, Oldham, and Stockport, developed from medium- to high-delinquency areas by a steep rise between 199 and 271 per cent. of their moderate pre-war delinquency. Among the pre-war low-delinquency areas which took part in the war and post-war increase by an exceedingly steep rise in their crime-rates, Norwich is the most spectacular illustration. By an unprecedented jump of 551 per cent., its crime-rate increased from 3·5 to 22·8 per 1,000 juveniles for three years. In this exceptional case the small pre-war figure qualifies the sensational percentage increase. Moreover, statistics alone cannot tell how adequately such unusual differences in court cases represent actual trends in criminality. Finally, the tentative character of the calculation of local population figures for juveniles must be taken into account. With these reservations, the figures in Table XI illustrate the fact that there are certain local variations not only in the rates of delinquency before and after the war, but also in the tempo and pace of the general upward trend of juvenile offences.

In order to understand the dynamics of the rise in crime in various groups of the population, one has to follow up the changing crime-rates from one year to another. Table XII shows the yearly rise and fall in the crime-rates for juvenile and adult males between 1938 and 1953. These figures suggest that the considerable increase in boys' delinquency is mainly due to the sharp rise in the first two years of the war, which has not been reversed by the post-war fall in 1946 and 1947 but is rather accentuated by the post-war peak of 1948. The crime-rate for men did not begin to rise until 1941; its increase in the year 1948 was less spectacular and its fall in the following year 1949 was more notable than the corresponding changes in the figures for boys.

There was a difference in the personal structure of juvenile delinquency in the various periods of increasing criminality. As Table XIII suggests, the steepest rise at the beginning of the war was among senior girls, while among boys the figures for juniors increased more sharply. By the end of the war the

TABLE XII. *Annual Increase in Crime of Boys 8–17 and Men 21 and Over, 1938–53*

Year	*Rate per 1,000 boys 8–17*	*Rate per 1,000 men 21 and over*
1938	9·2	2·3
1939	10·4	2·1
1940	14·3	1·9
1941	14·5	2·6
1942	13·3	2·8
1943	13·7	2·8
1944	14·4	2·8
1945	15·7	3·1
1946	13·3	3·1
1947	12·6	3·8
1948	15·9	4·1
1949	14·7	3·5
1950	15·3	3·5
1951	16·8	4·2
1952	15·4	4·2
1953	13·4	4·1

TABLE XIII. *Increase in Juvenile Crime in Three Periods*

Year	*Rate of delinquency per 1,000*	*Increase or decrease*	*Percentage increase or decrease*	*Rate of delinquency per 1,000*	*Increase or decrease*	*Percentage increase or decrease*
			Children			
	Boys			*Girls*		
1939	9·30			0·55		
1940	13·04	3·74	40·2	0·83	0·30	56
1944	13·3			0·94		
1945	13·6	0·3	2·2	0·92	—0·02	—2·5
1947	11·4			0·96		
1948	14·3	2·9	25·4	1·23	0·27	28·1
			Young Persons			
	Boys			*Girls*		
1939	12·48			0·91		
1940	16·74	4·26	34·1	1·58	0·67	73·5
1944	16·5			2·11		
1945	19·7	3·2	29·0	1·99	—0·12	—5·7
1947	15·2			1·78		
1948	19·0	3·8	25·4	2·12	0·34	19·0

rise affected the senior boys to a greater degree than the other groups. The post-war peak of 1948 was the result of an almost equal rise in the crime-rates of junior and senior boys and junior girls.

Like most other criminological studies the preceding observations on rising and falling tendencies in juvenile delinquency

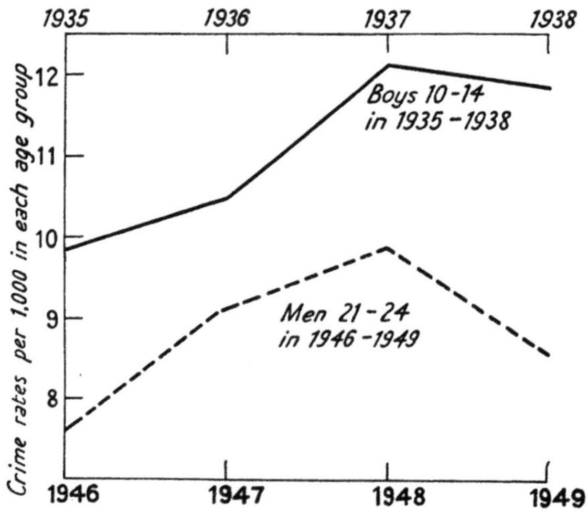

Fig. 1. Crime-curve of two age groups: boys 10–14 in years 1935–8; men 21–24 in years 1946–9.

were based on an analysis of the rates of persons found guilty at certain places and within certain periods. Such an approach does not take into account how far the juvenile delinquents of a certain time and place are newcomers to crime or boys and girls who have come before the courts once more after previous criminal experience. Crime and delinquency should not only be described in terms of yearly convictions without consideration of the past of the offenders, but should also be seen as an impact on the career of individuals and thus as something which affects the life of a generation. Some of the children who were born during the depression of the early thirties and were evacuated during the war appeared before the courts as delinquent young persons in the post-war years, while boys and girls born during the war were some of the school-children who filled the ranks of post-war delinquency. As far as statistical evidence is available, Fig. 1 illustrates the impact of crime on a generation. The upper curve represents delinquency-rates for boys aged 10–14 for the years 1935–8, and the lower one represents crime-rates for men aged 21–24 for 1946–9. Between the two curves there is thus a time-lag of ten years. A comparison of the two curves allows of two conclusions. On the one hand, there is a considerable distance between them. This means that a notable proportion of juvenile delinquents does not appear before the court as adult offenders. On the other hand, both curves move in almost completely parallel directions. When the curve of juvenile delinquency rises, ten years later the curve of adult crime rises as well, and vice versa. It appears that the rising numbers of adult offenders belong to a generation which had been affected by an increase in juvenile delinquency.

The Social Setting of High-delinquency Areas

Juvenile delinquency is not an isolated factor in the life of the community. It is therefore pertinent to study the crime situation in high-delinquency areas in conjunction with other facts which are characteristic of the social and economic conditions in a particular district. The geographical distribution of high-delinquency and low-delinquency areas suggests that delinquency-rates are high in large, densely populated communities. Map 2 illustrates this point. It shows the situation of high-delinquency areas in relation to various degrees of density of population in England and Wales. With the exception of the West Riding of Yorkshire, which presents special population problems to be discussed later, all high-delinquency areas consist of, or are situated in, the most densely populated localities. At the same time, as is always the case in a study of the causes of crime, this observation does not justify a proposition which could stand the test of cross-examination. As the map shows, there are equally densely populated localities which are not high-delinquency areas.

In most places with a high rate of juvenile delinquency there is apparent evidence of extensive criminal activities in general. In 1938, in the country as a whole, the number of indictable offences known to the police was 8 per 1,000 of the population of 8 years and over. In 1950 this figure had risen to 12. Of those

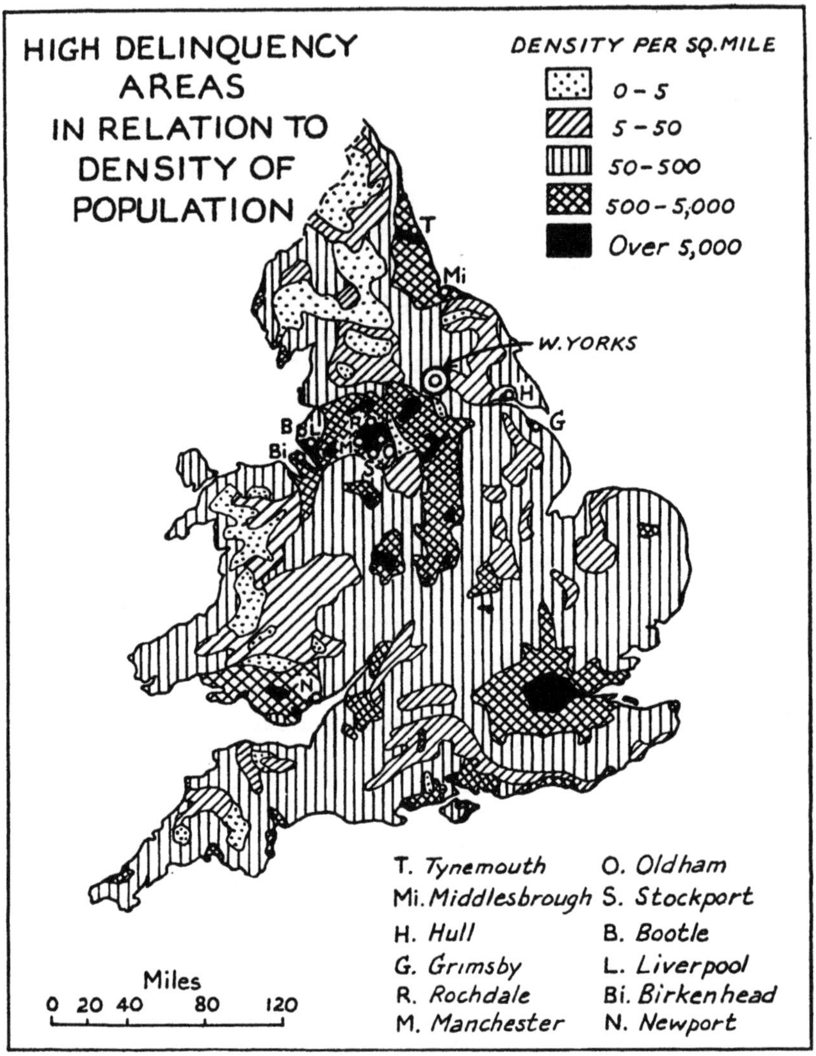
HIGH DELINQUENCY AREAS IN RELATION TO DENSITY OF POPULATION
DENSITY PER SQ. MILE
0 – 5
5 – 50
50 – 500
500 – 5,000
Over 5,000
T
Mi
W. YORKS
H
G
B
Bi
N
T. Tynemouth
Mi. Middlesbrough
H. Hull
G. Grimsby
R. Rochdale
M. Manchester
O. Oldham
S. Stockport
B. Bootle
L. Liverpool
Bi. Birkenhead
N. Newport
Miles
0 20 40 80 120

Map 2

places which were high-delinquency areas both before and after the war, Manchester had, in 1950, a general rate of crime known to the police of 23·9, Liverpool of 23·6, and Birkenhead of 19·7. Grimsby, with a crime rate of 16·6, and Bootle, of 16·7, were still markedly above the national mean. In Tyneside, South Shields and Gateshead had moderate crime-rates both before and after the war. Their rates of juvenile delinquency were considerable before the war, but from this high standard they increased only moderately. At the same time, in Newcastle and Tynemouth, both the rates of crime known to the police and juvenile delinquency increased considerably. The rates of crime known to the police rose from 7·0 and 5·4 respectively to 14·0 and 12·4. The rates of juvenile delinquency for the same localities increased from 14·7 and 13·1 for the three-year period 1936–8 to 31·2 and 44·3 for the period 1948–50. In Tynemouth local inquiries showed that there had been no change in the methods of recording crimes or in the practice of cautioning or prosecuting juvenile offenders. The rising delinquency-rates must therefore be regarded as an indication of an increase in actual delinquency. Observers on the spot attribute this development to a large-scale erection of new housing estates on the outskirts of the town where so far there has been little provision for community centres and play parks. Groups of boys between 11 and 15 years, dissatisfied with the dull and quiet atmosphere of their new environment, are attracted by the light and amusement of the town centre, and there find themselves easily involved in stealing from vehicles and taking other people's bicycles. Since the total population of Tynemouth remained stable, increasing numbers of young law-breakers led to steeply rising delinquency-rates. However, even with this interpretation, the high delinquency-rates for boys of tender years remain unexplained. While senior boys exceed the average delinquency-rate of their age group by 38·7 per 1,000, juniors surpass their average delinquency-rate by 42·6.

A close association between crime in general and juvenile delinquency in particular may be due to one of two reasons. Where many adults are inclined to commit criminal offences, juveniles follow their example. At the same time, where a large number of juveniles are concerned in stealing, many cases of loss of property and of alleged breaking and entering are reported and swell the numbers of crimes known to the police. There are, however, places with a different pattern. At Hull the rate of crimes known to the police fell from 12·9 in 1938 (a figure which was in excess of the national mean) to 11·8 in 1950, thus corresponding to the average for the whole country. During the same period Hull developed from a high-average-delinquency area before the war with a juvenile delinquency-rate of 20·7 to a high-delinquency area after the war with a delinquency-rate of 38·4. Middlesbrough, with a general crime-rate of 9·3 before the war and of 11·5 after the war, and thus in both periods near the national mean, was a high-delinquency area almost at the top of the list with a rate of 48·2 per 1,000 in 1936–8 and 55·6 in 1948–50.

These facts may be interpreted in either of two ways. At first glance they seem to suggest that Hull and Middlesbrough are specific delinquency areas where juvenile offenders, or at least the court appearances of juvenile offenders, are more significant than the crime situation in general. However, an explanation of the low figures of crimes known to the police in these two places may also be found in a more selective method of registration by the police. In Hull, before the Stipendiary Magistrate, adults of 21 and over were found guilty of indictable offences at a rate of 1·3 per 1,000 in 1938 and 2·1 in 1950. Compared with the corresponding figures in the whole country for adults before magistrates' courts, which were 1·1 in 1938 and 1·5 in 1950, the figures for Hull indicate a considerable increase in adult crime in spite of the fall in police figures. Likewise in Middlesbrough the almost normal rates of crime known to the police coincided not only with substantially high delinquency rates but also with rates of adult offenders before the Stipendiary Magistrate which amounted to 1·4 in 1938 and 2·2 in 1950 and were therefore in both periods above the national mean. In the light of these figures both places show, not so much a difference between the crime situation in general and the amount of juvenile delinquency in particular, but between a comparatively moderate rate of crimes known to the police, on the one hand, and relatively high conviction rates for juveniles and adults alike, on the other. In the course of the discussion which follows, further evidence will be produced which allows of some conclusions in the question whether this discrepancy is due to specific local delinquency problems or has to be explained by the methods of registration by the police.

The fact that juvenile delinquency is most frequent in big industrial centres is further illustrated by other aspects of the social situation in characteristic high-delinquency areas. The One-per-cent. Sample of the Census of 1951 shows that for England and Wales as a whole 30 per cent. of the male population occupied or retired are engaged in only partly skilled or in unskilled occupations. Among the six outstanding high-delinquency areas, Bootle, Middlesbrough, and Grimsby have as many as 44 per cent. of their men engaged in partly skilled or unskilled occupations, Tynemouth follows with 40 per cent., and Liverpool and Birkenhead with 35 and 34 respectively. It has been further shown in a recent statistical investigation that the 'social class of towns' can be determined by the estimated percentage of households in which, in 1950, the chief wage-earner earned at least £7. 10*s.* per week. Estimated figures for wages and salaries in 130 towns in England and Wales showed that 18 was the average percentage of such households in these towns. The poorest of the places under observation were Rhondda and the small Lancashire town of Widnes with a rate of only 6 per cent., the most prosperous the south coast resorts of Eastbourne and Bournemouth with rates of 33 and 38 per cent. respectively. In the light of these figures, delinquency is most significant not in small and very poor districts but in large towns with a predominance of small incomes. Among the six most characteristic high-delinquency areas, Bootle and Middlesbrough have households with an income of at least £7. 10*s.* at a rate of no more than 9 and 10 per cent. respectively; Liverpool and Birkenhead at a rate of 14 per cent.; and only Grimsby and Manchester correspond to the average percentage with figures of 18 and 19 respectively.[1]

One might have expected that a growing influx of population into centres of industry would prove one of the factors which explain high delinquency-rates. However, as shown above, a comparison between population and delinquency trends in industrial and rural areas makes such an hypothesis improbable. Further evidence suggests that there has been less internal migration in the direction of the big cities than one might

[1] L. T. Wilkins, *Applied Statistics* (1952), No. 1, pp. 27–33.

have thought, and that the high-delinquency areas are places where the population has been remarkably stable. According to the *Preliminary Report of the Census of 1951*, the large provincial conurbations of Merseyside, Tyneside, south-east Lancashire, and west Yorkshire, which include the principal high-delinquency areas, have had stable population figures for the last twenty years. This consistency in population figures is not a mere statistical phenomenon, but the expression of an actual stability in the population. Further Census figures show that in the East and West Ridings and in the north-western region these constant population figures are not the result of immigrants making good the losses of a falling birth-rate, but, on the contrary, of a birth-rate exceeding the percentage of deaths and thus compensating for loss by migration. Of the big provincial conurbations, only the west Midlands increased their population on account of an additional gain by migration of 5 per cent.[1] At the same time, the crime situation in Birmingham differs notably from Tyneside and Merseyside. The rates of crime known to the police were 7·5 in 1938 and 12·1 in 1950, thus corresponding closely to the national mean. The three-year rates of juvenile delinquency were 19·2 before and 33·8 after the war. This means that juvenile delinquency in Birmingham has risen in a way that is almost parallel to the trend in the whole country. Birmingham was, and has remained, only a high-average-delinquency area. On the whole the impression prevails that internal migration moves from big industrial centres to the adjacent countryside which takes the overflow of urban population.[2] This fact throws some light on the surprising experience that rural districts have a high rate of adolescent crime.

The question of the contribution rendered by immigrants to the ranks of juvenile offenders in high-delinquency areas needs further elucidation. It would be most instructive if the proportion of persons born in their place of residence could be obtained for comparable groups of offenders and non-offenders. Short of such special investigation, it must be assumed that the 'flight from the country' is not a predominant cause of urban juvenile delinquency.

[1] General Register Office, *Census 1951, England and Wales, Preliminary Report, 1951*, Table G at p. xv and Table J at p. xxii.

[2] M. P. Newton and J. R. Jeffery, *Internal Migration*, H.M.S.O., 1951.

Juvenile delinquency is not the only symptom of social maladjustment. For an illustration of this fact, local variations in delinquency were compared with the geographical distribution of infant mortality. For the three years under observation, 1948–50, the mortality-rate of infants in the first year of life was 32 per 1,000 live births in England and Wales, but of the thirteen high-delinquency areas only one, Grimsby, with a rate of 30, was below the national mean. Stockport, West Riding, Tynemouth, and Newport had infant mortality-rates between 37 and 39, and the other eight high-delinquency areas had rates between 40 in Hull and 51 in Bootle.[1] Rates of juvenile delinquency are therefore associated in some degree with the figures for infant mortality. This observation does not exclude the possibility of specific infant mortality areas, where excessive mortality-rates are more significant than juvenile delinquency or other symptoms of social maladjustment. Rotherham, Sunderland, and Warrington have infant mortality-rates of more than 50, while they are not outstanding in juvenile delinquency.

An investigation of crime conditions in different places is confronted with the same difficulties which beset a study of causes and factors of crime among individual offenders. The more research is concerned with concrete characteristics, the less possible it seems to support any general statements. Attempts at classification and typology break down before the uniqueness and endless variety of human life. Social ecology, the study of the topographical distribution of social phenomena, is still in its initial stages. It is too early to work out the prevalence of factors connected with crime and delinquency in different localities in terms of statistical correlations. With these reservations, however, certain characteristic patterns of high-delinquency areas emerge. Like factors of individual criminality, they neither apply to all cases with the same criminological diagnosis, nor are they associated with a high incidence of crime alone. They are illustrations rather than symptoms which have the infallible strength of a natural law. The characteristic pattern of a high-delinquency area is a big industrial town with the typical social structure of an industrial population, not a place where poverty is prevalent, but where there is a

[1] Registrar-General, *Statistical Review of England and Wales*, Part II, Civil, 1948, Table E, p. 11; 1949, Table E, p. 10; 1950, Table E, p. 10.

high proportion of small incomes, where there is considerable infant mortality, though not necessarily with the highest infant mortality rates. High-delinquency areas are often places with a significant criminality in general. Contrary to what one would expect, high-delinquency areas are districts where there is, over a considerable number of years, a consistency in high-delinquency rates within a stable population.

If one goes farther back in the history of crime in England one finds certain observations in respect of local variations in juvenile delinquency under the impact of depression and unemployment between the two wars. According to the Introduction to *Criminal Statistics for 1929*, the number of persons found guilty of indictable offences rose between 1921 and 1929 by 34 per cent. in the north of England against 24 per cent. in the south of England. Thus the number of crimes committed in the north exceeded those of the south in 1929 even more markedly than in 1921, while according to the distribution of population only 165 crimes in the north were to be expected for every 253 in the south. At the same time, the share of juveniles among offenders was 25·9 of the high figure in the north and 18·1 of the low figure in the south. The same difference was reflected in the qualitative structure of juvenile delinquency. More than every second of the numerous cases of juvenile delinquency in the north, 56·2 per cent., was shop-breaking, against 37·8 per cent. of the less numerous cases in the south.

The relation between juvenile unemployment and delinquency during the depression of the 1930's has been carefully investigated by Dr. Mannheim.[1] While he did not find in every place a rise in juvenile unemployment followed by an increase in juvenile delinquency, he came to the conclusion that when and where both curves run parallel the rise in delinquency was to be attributed to the mounting unemployment. In the light of the further experience of the present survey, the evidence seems to emphasize a rather independent trend in juvenile delinquency. In Table XIV unemployment rates for nine places shown in Dr. Mannheim's study are compared with delinquency-rates computed from his figures and with those of the present survey. South Shields and Gateshead were hard

[1] H. Mannheim, *Social Aspects of Crime in England* (Allen & Unwin, 1940), pp. 136–43.

hit by unemployment, had high delinquency-rates, and are still high-delinquency areas. The same picture of high delinquency then and now is characteristic of Liverpool which had

TABLE XIV. *Juvenile Unemployment and Delinquency in Selected Areas*

Area	*Percentage unemployment rate, 1934–6*	*Delinquency-rate, 1934–6*	*Delinquency-rate, 1948–50*
Liverpool . .	29·8	40·7	55·0
S. Shields . .	68·8	28·6	30·2
Gateshead . .	56·8	23·5	36·8
Manchester . .	9·3	19·0	40·5
Merthyr Tydvil .	63·5	17·5	27·4
Birmingham . .	1·5	15·3	33·8
Leeds . . .	2·8	14·2	32·6
Sheffield . .	11·0	8·4	17·6
Norwich . .	6·1	4·2	20·4

(*Acknowledgement is made to Dr. H. Mannheim and to Messrs. Allen & Unwin for permission to use certain figures in* Social Aspects of Crime *in the compilation of this table.*)

a surprisingly low rate of unemployment. At the same time Merthyr Tydvil had and still has a medium delinquency-rate in spite of much unemployment in the 'thirties.

Effects of Preventive Efforts: Police and Child Care

The difficulty of isolating certain potential crime factors and determining their specific significance as causes of juvenile delinquency arises again if one tries to weigh the influence of the forces intended to prevent delinquency and to reduce crime. This applies to the work of the police and to child care. In an area with normal delinquency-rates a strong police force would be expected to reduce the extent of juvenile delinquency by their preventive work, but at the same time to increase the number of court cases by more frequent prosecutions. In other districts a high delinquency-rate may be the reason for increasing the police force, while the sheer magnitude of the numbers of crimes reported puts a limit to the possible rate of offences detected and offenders brought before the court. Of the six outstanding high-delinquency areas, four have a police force stronger than the mean rate for the boroughs of England and

Wales. The average picture in an English or Welsh borough is that 605 people are looked after by one policeman. At Grimsby the corresponding figure is 565; at Bootle 550; Birkenhead 517; in Liverpool there is even one policeman for every 399 persons in the population. At the same time, Tynemouth, which only recently appeared to be more conspicuous as a place of considerable delinquency in Tyneside, has a relatively smaller police force of one officer for every 625 inhabitants, and Middlesbrough, where a moderate general crime-rate coincides with a high rate of juvenile delinquency, has even 657 persons looked after by one policeman. Results of police work do not depend on the numerical strength of the police force in relation to the size of the local population alone. The distances which have to be covered, facilities for transport and communication, and emphasis laid on the prevention of crime or on the detection of offenders, influence the outcome of the work of the police. Statistical calculation confirms the view that the detection-rate does not depend on the strength of the police force alone. For all municipal boroughs in the country there is a correlation of +0·24 between a high number of policemen per local inhabitants and a low rate of crimes cleared up.[1]

Local detection-rates are, however, important for the interpretation of the figures for juveniles found guilty before the courts. Where only a moderate fraction of crimes reported to the police is cleared up, a high delinquency-rate appears even more formidable. A high detection-rate suggests that even large numbers of court cases may represent a relatively small amount of actual lawlessness. From this point of view juvenile delinquency in Merseyside reveals itself in its full significance. In 1952 the mean detection-rate for all police districts in England and Wales based on the number of districts was 55. At the same time, the local detection-rate for Birkenhead was 53, Bootle 46, and Liverpool 32. In all these places, as stated above, the rate of crimes known to the police considerably exceeds the national mean. The general crime-rate for Liverpool is almost twice as high as that for the country as a whole. It thus appears that

[1] Institute of Municipal Treasurers and Accountants/Society of County Treasurers, *Police Force Statistics 1952/3*. The figures in the text above are calculated from those given in this source, though taking as the basis for the mean rate for boroughs the number of boroughs instead of the total population in the boroughs. Local detection-rates are computed from figures provided by the Home Office.

court figures in Liverpool are only a modest fraction of a comparatively large amount of criminality. The actual number of juvenile offenders in Merseyside must be assumed to exceed by far even the high number of court cases. All this leads to the conclusion that the delinquency-rates for Liverpool, Birkenhead, and Bootle represent indeed a considerable amount of juvenile delinquency.

In Middlesbrough a similar interpretation of statistical evidence leads to a different result. In the discussion above, Middlesbrough was characterized as a place of 'specific' juvenile delinquency, that is to say, a place where a normal general crime-rate of 11·5 crimes known to the police per 1,000 inhabitants coincides with a high delinquency-rate of 55·6 for three years. At the same time this discrepancy might at least partly be explained by a more selective method of recording crimes known to the police. In Middlesbrough the local police force has a strength of one policeman for every 657 inhabitants and claims a detection-rate of 74 per cent. This unusually high rate of crimes cleared up corroborates the evidence which suggests that the police in Middlesbrough are rather selective in recording alleged offences as crimes known to the police. Such an assumption does not rule out the possibility that Middlesbrough would still have a high detection-rate even if crimes were recorded in the same way as elsewhere. In any case, a high detection-rate affects the significance of high-delinquency figures. It means that the number of court cases represents an unusually high proportion of the actual offences committed and thus includes cases which elsewhere are hidden in the unknown 'dark figure' of criminal statistics. This possibility must, in fairness, be taken into account since Middlesbrough has been listed as an outstanding high-delinquency area.[1]

Hull, another 'specific' high-delinquency area, shows a different picture. It has a high delinquency-rate of 38·4 in the face of a moderate rate of crimes known to the police of 11·8, and a not unusually high detection-rate of 50. If one applies the same considerations which were used in the interpretation of the Middlesbrough figures, it seems reasonable to assume that, in the light of a rather normal detection-rate, the moderate

[1] For a general background of social conditions and social work in Middlesbrough see Ruth Glass, *Social Background of a Plan, A Study of Middlesbrough*, 1948.

crime-rate represents the real crime situation. Consequently, the high rates of juvenile delinquency and of adult convictions in Hull suggest that the amount of crime is in fact considerable and cannot be explained as the result of a mere technical enumeration of court decisions inflated by numerous cases which elsewhere escape detection and prosecution.

The relation between the extent of child care and the amount of juvenile delinquency is more difficult to determine than the effects of the preventive work of the police. One would expect that places with high numbers of court cases would have many children under the care of the Children's Officer, but one might also assume that an intense system of child care has the healthy effect of preventing a good deal of juvenile delinquency. In 1952, at one date, the rate of children in care per 1,000 children under the age of 18 in county boroughs of England and Wales was 6·3. In Merseyside the rates of children under care in Bootle and Birkenhead were 3·9 and 4·6 respectively and are thus considerably below the general mean, while Liverpool, with more than three-quarters of a million inhabitants, has a high rate of 7·9. Manchester, another high-delinquency town, with a population of more than 700,000, has an even higher rate of 8·3. Middlesbrough with 5·8 and Grimsby with 6·6 are high-delinquency areas where rates of children under care more or less correspond to the average for county boroughs.[1] As far as this evidence goes the effects of child care are not yet reflected in the figures of criminal statistics. High-delinquency areas include places with low, medium, and, in large cities, with high rates of cases under the care of the Children's Officer.

Conclusions

The observations discussed in this chapter reveal the picture of juvenile delinquency as it confronts the courts. As a result the following features seem to be characteristic of the present situation.

1. Out of 1,000 juveniles 25·2 were found guilty of indictable offences during the three-year period 1948–50.

2. The specific delinquency-rates were highest, 51·0 per 1,000

[1] Institute of Municipal Treasurers and Accountants/Society of County Treasurers, *Children Services Statistics 1952/3*. See also *Children in the Care of Local Authorities*, H.M.S.O., 1954, Cmd. 9145.

for senior boys, less high, 39·0, among junior boys, owing to the small number of delinquents among boys between 8 and 9. Among senior girls and junior girls the rate is notably lower, 6·5 and 3·4 respectively.

3. A comparison between police districts in England and Wales shows thirteen high-delinquency areas, covering a juvenile population of 539,471 with a delinquency-rate of more than 37 per 1,000, and seventeen low-delinquency areas covering a juvenile population of 370,798, with a delinquency-rate of less than 13 per 1,000.

4. Heading the list of high-delinquency areas is Bootle owing to the exceedingly high delinquency-rate for senior boys of 118·9. The second and third places in the order of high delinquency, Middlesbrough and Birkenhead, have high delinquency-rates for all four age and sex groups.

5. A comparison of the three-year delinquency-rates for the country as a whole for 1936–8 with the corresponding rates for 1948–50 shows an increase from 4·0 to 6·2 for adults, from 12·6 to 17·4 for adolescents, and from 14·3 to 25·5 for juveniles.

6. Among male offenders the comparison between juveniles and adults shows that for boys there was a steeper rise in the first two years of the war and during the post-war peak year of 1948, and a less notable fall in the receding criminality of 1949.

7. There is a relative consistency with regard to areas with the most intense delinquency both before and after the war. Bootle, Middlesbrough, Birkenhead, and Liverpool, with a post-war delinquency-rate of 55 and more, were high-delinquency areas before the war.

8. The rise in the average figure for juvenile delinquency in 132 police districts, as it is indicated by a comparison between a pre-war and a post-war triennium, is mainly due to a moderate increase of criminal activities in the high-delinquency areas, Grimsby, Birkenhead, and Bootle, and a steep rise in the hitherto medium-delinquency areas of Tynemouth, Rochdale, Oldham, and Stockport.

9. There is no evidence that other unfavourable social conditions are always associated with high rates of juvenile delinquency and only prevalent in high-delinquency areas, but there emerges a certain pattern which characterizes typical high-delinquency areas. Such places are mostly large manufacturing

towns or ports with the usual structure of an industrial population, a high proportion of small incomes, considerable though not excessive infant mortality, and with a significant adult criminality.

10. High delinquency-rates are not associated with growing figures of urban population which increase by a continuous influx of newcomers, but are rather characteristic of places which have maintained over a number of years a comparatively stable population.

These observations illustrate the general features of juvenile delinquency in England and Wales, both in respect of its local distribution throughout the country and of its trend from pre-war years throughout the war years to the post-war period. The facts brought to light by the preceding discussion determine the task with which the magistrates have been concerned.

CHAPTER III

THE TREATMENT PRACTICE OF THE COURTS IN DIFFERENT PARTS OF THE COUNTRY

Local Rates of Different Forms of Treatment

English juvenile courts, as it has been pointed out in the introductory chapter, have three possibilities in dealing with juvenile offenders. The magistrates may take no action at all and discharge the young offender absolutely or conditionally. They may feel that constructive treatment, either institutional or non-institutional, is necessary, and, for this reason, put the offender on probation or commit him to the care of a fit person or to an Approved School. Alternatively, they may resort to punishment and fine him, send him to an Attendance Centre, order detention in a Remand Home, or, more recently, commit him to a Detention Centre. If, for the last age group under their jurisdiction, those between 16 and 17, a sentence of Borstal training is, in the opinion of the court, advisable, the offender has to be committed to Quarter Sessions. With regard to non-offenders, the same constructive, educative measures are applicable as for offenders. Table I showed how English juvenile courts made use of their powers in a typical post-war year, and Table II indicated certain differences in the treatment practice before and after the war. The courts' preference for one or the other form of treatment differs in respect of the age and sex of the offender. Table XV illustrates, for the country as a whole, the application of various forms of treatment to four different groups of delinquents in the three-year span 1948–50. Probation orders are still the largest single group among the courts' decisions. Among girls every second one is put on probation. As one would expect, absolute discharge is more frequently used for juniors than for seniors, while the application of conditional discharge is more evenly spread among all four groups. Among delinquents the highest rate of committals to Approved Schools applies to senior boys. Fit person orders are only sparingly used for offenders. More than three out of four juveniles committed to the care of a fit person are non-offenders deemed to be in need of care and protection. The highest incidence of fines occurs among senior boys who may have to pay them out of their own pockets.

TABLE XV. *National Rates of Treatment applied by Juvenile Courts in dealing with Indictable Offenders, 1948–50*

Method of treatment	*Percentage of offenders dealt with in each age and sex group*				*Percentage of offenders dealt with among all juveniles 8–17*
	Boys 8–13	*Boys 14–17*	*Girls 8–13*	*Girls 14–17*	
Absolute discharge	24·4	15·8	24·8	13·9	21·0
Conditional discharge	10·9	9·5	8·5	8·8	10·0
Probation	41·2	40·9	47·9	54·4	41·4
Committed to the care of a fit person	1·4	0·5	0·4	0·1	1·3
Approved Schools	6·6	11·1	5·7	8·2	8·4
Fines	13·7	17·7	8·0	10·6	14·6
Otherwise dealt with	1·8	4·5	4·7	4·0	3·3

All these observations refer to national figures which express the experience of the country as a whole. However, just as there is a geography of crime with certain high-delinquency and certain low-delinquency areas, so, in the field of treatment, the preference for certain measures and the reluctance to use other ways of dealing with delinquents vary between different places and districts. For the study of local differences in judicial treatment practice, the discussion which follows deals with five methods of treatment, absolute discharge, conditional discharge, probation, Approved Schools, and fines, in their application to indictable offences committed by boys of 8 and under 14 years, boys of 14 and under 17, girls of 8 and under 14, and girls of 14 and under 17. Unfortunately, committals to the care of a fit person had to be omitted. Although this form of treatment is most significant in view of its recent development under the Children Act, 1948, and the growing experience of Children's Officers, in many of the less densely populated districts the number of relevant cases was too small to allow of any statistical evaluation. The presentation of material collected with the intention of throwing light on the application of different modes of treatment to different types of delinquents by a great number of different courts is not feasible without a rigid restriction of the field of inquiry. The calculation of correlations between too many different sets of figures would lead to a confusing number of combinations. The present study concentrates therefore on five forms of treatment in respect of four groups of juvenile offenders followed up through each district of England and Wales.

At first glance, variations in treatment practice seem to be less significant than one had expected. Table XVI suggests that four-fifths of the juvenile population of England and Wales are under the jurisdiction of courts where the magistrates use the five different methods of treatment in a way which more or less corresponds to the average picture drawn from the figures for all police districts in the country. This picture is to be supplemented by a study of districts with non-typical treatment practice. In the use of absolute and conditional discharge and of probation, the exceptions are more significant in the direction of a less frequent use of these methods, while for Approved Schools and fines the reverse is true, since juveniles in districts with a frequent resort to these measures outnumber those who are under the jurisdiction of courts where magistrates are reluctant to fine a young law-breaker or to commit him to an Approved School. As far as the number of juveniles at risk are concerned, the exceptions to the rule point to a more severe treatment rather than an unwarranted leniency towards young offenders.

For a comparative study, the numbers of juveniles under jurisdictions where the treatment practice conforms to the average of all districts or deviates from it give a preliminary orientation only. For any further elucidation these differences should not only be assessed at the receiving end, but must also be studied with a view to the courts which award the different forms of treatment. A comparison of the small figures for particular forms of treatment in the juvenile courts of the thousand-odd petty sessional divisions is not feasible. The basic unit therefore for the present research is once more the individual police district. The figures in the third column in Table XVI show that differences in treatment practice are not only reflected in the proportions of the juvenile population at risk, but also in the numbers of districts where one or the other treatment policy prevails. Each method of approach gives a different impression of the general use of probation. There are more juveniles under the jurisdiction of courts with a less frequent

TABLE XVI. *Methods of Treatment as practised in Various Parts of the Country, 1948–50*

Treatment	*Degree of use*	*Number of districts*	*Juvenile population*	*Percentage of juvenile population*
Absolute discharge	Frequent .	11	417,000	8·3
	Normal .	99	4,104,000	81·7
	Infrequent	22	503,000	10·0
		132	5,024,000	100·0
Conditional discharge	Frequent .	13	250,000	4·9
	Normal .	92	4,314,000	85·9
	Infrequent	27	460,000	9·2
		132	5,024,000	100·0
Probation	Frequent .	8	117,000	2·3
	Normal .	115	4,520,000	90·0
	Infrequent	9	387,000	7·7
		132	5,024,000	100·0
Approved Schools	Frequent .	10	138,000	2·7
	Normal .	121	4,867,000	96·9
	Infrequent	1	19,000	0·4
		132	5,024,000	100·0
Fines	Frequent .	16	513,000	10·2
	Normal .	105	4,243,000	84·7
	Infrequent	11	268,000	5·1
		132	5,024,000	100·0

The figures for normal, frequent, and infrequent use have been calculated by taking the mean for all districts as normal and adding or subtracting the standard deviation.

use of probation than with a more frequent use, but in terms of police districts concerned deviations from the average proportion of probation orders are more evenly spread. The number of districts with a more generous or a less frequent use of probation is almost the same, but the nine districts with infrequent probation orders cover a much larger juvenile population than the eight districts where the courts frequently apply probation.

This last observation shows the importance of a topographical distribution of differences in judicial treatment practice. From an administrative point of view it would be valuable to know which are high-probation and low-probation areas and so forth. Such knowledge makes it possible to study a certain treatment practice in the light of local delinquency patterns and other social conditions and to compare the experience which courts have gained of different methods applied to comparable cases of juvenile delinquency. For this purpose, certain standards of rates of the different forms of treatment awarded by the courts were established beyond which a frequent use could be assessed as a high rate and an infrequent use as a low rate of each particular method.[1] Table XVII shows the districts which made a notably high or markedly low use of the five particular forms of treatment under observation. These districts were selected on the strength of aggregate figures for the type of treatment awarded to juveniles of both sexes and all age groups as indicated in the last column. The geographical distribution of one outstanding characteristic of treatment practice is illustrated by Map 3. There is a belt of districts with high rates of fines stretching through the north Midlands and parts of the industrial areas in the north-east. As Table XVII shows, in most of these areas a high incidence of fines coincides with a low incidence of absolute discharge. At the same time, the geographical distribution of variations in probation gives the impression of more or less accidental deviations from a widespread common practice.

The classification of districts according to high or low rates of the application of certain forms of treatment to juvenile delinquents of all ages and both sexes involves a generalization. In fact such figures are numerical averages which may cover considerable differences. A high rate of a particular form of treatment in a district may mean that magistrates favour this

[1] Standards of a high or low use of a particular form of treatment refer to treatment-rates for the aggregate juvenile population of 8–17 years.

They are:

For absolute discharge . .	Above 31·6	and below 7·6	per cent.
„ conditional discharge .	„ 17·8	„ „ 4·0	„
„ probation . . .	„ 71.0	„ „ 20.5	„
„ Approved Schools . .	„ 15·3	„ „ 4·0	„
„ fines	„ 28·2	„ „ 4·5	„

TABLE XVII. *Districts with High and Low Rates of Five Methods of Treatment*

ABSOLUTE DISCHARGE

District	*Boys 8–13*	*Boys 14–17*	*Girls 8–13*	*Girls 14–17*	*Aggregate juvenile population 8–17*
		High rate of application of treatment			
CARMARTHENSHIRE	57·0	30·9	43·6	42·8	48·9
Newcastle	49·8	35·0	31·6	33·3	44·5
Merthyr Tydvil	48·4	35·1	83·3	16·0	43·0
GLAMORGANSHIRE	48·1	30·7	51·8	30·7	39·5
Swansea	43·5	24·3	28·6	35·3	37·1
YORKSHIRE W.	40·8	25·4	45·4	17·4	35·8
CARDIGANSHIRE	39·4	28·0	50·0	—	34·3
Newport (Mon.)	38·1	21·0	68·7	23·1	34·1
CAERNARVONSHIRE	34·2	36·5	14·3	25·0	33·3
Burnley	32·6	34·4	31·5	11·1	32·2
		Low rate of application of treatment			
Huddersfield	0·5	1·9	—	—	0·9
Cambridge	2·8	—	—	—	1·0
Halifax	2·9	2·9	—	—	2·5
DEVONSHIRE	2·9	3·9	5·3	2·7	3·4
RUTLANDSHIRE	7·7	—	—	—	3·7
Hastings	4·6	5·9	—	—	4·4
HUNTINGDONSHIRE	8·1	2·0	—	—	4·3
Bolton	2·6	8·5	—	—	4·5
Oxford	5·9	3·2	9·0	10·0	4·1
Preston	6·0	3·2	9·5	11·1	5·3

The following districts made no use of absolute discharge: MERIONETHSHIRE, St. Helens, Worcester.

TABLE XVII. *Districts with High and Low Rates of Five Methods of Treatment (cont.)*

CONDITIONAL DISCHARGE

District	*Boys 8–13*	*Boys 14–17*	*Girls 8–13*	*Girls 14–17*	*Aggregate juvenile population 8–17*
		High rate of application of treatment			
Southampton	32·2	20·8	35·3	15·4	28·5
Preston	24·3	20·2	47·6	22·2	24·2
Southport	28·6	23·4	—	—	23·6
Bristol	28·3	14·4	32·9	17·6	23·3
Tynemouth	21·5	26·8	11·1	—	22·6
Barrow-in-Furness	22·3	18·1	46·7	20·0	22·1
Warrington	25·7	14·2	26·1	8·3	21·2
Manchester	21·7	20·6	23·6	21·3	21·5
Doncaster	21·4	17·1	16·7	28·6	20·0
Wigan	22·6	12·5	—	—	19·2
Worcester	20·6	18·2	—	20·0	19·2
MID-WALES	17·2	22·6	—	—	19·1
		Low rate of application of treatment			
Birkenhead	0·2	0·7	—	—	0·03
Exeter	0·6	—	—	—	0·4
Sunderland	0·3	1·3	—	—	0·6
Derby	—	3·2	—	—	0·9
Wallasey	0·9	2·2	—	—	1·1
Halifax	0·7	1·9	—	—	1·1
Birmingham	1·3	1·2	2·3	1·0	1·2
ANGLESEY	3·2	—	—	—	1·5
Gt. Yarmouth	—	2·9	—	14·3	1·7

The following districts made no use of conditional discharge: Burnley, Eastbourne.

TABLE XVII. *Districts with High and Low Rates of Five Methods of Treatment (cont.)*

PROBATION

District	Boys 8–13	Boys 14–17	Girls 8–13	Girls 14–17	Aggregate juvenile population 8–17
	High rate of application of treatment				
MERIONETHSHIRE	95·0	66·7	100·0	—	79·2
Halifax	79·2	74·8	78·7	100·0	78·3
Huddersfield	79·3	67·6	80·8	71·4	75·4
	Low rate of application of treatment				
Swansea	14·0	12·1	47·5	29·4	14·8
Rotherham	12·0	13·0	25·0	46·1	14·8
YORKSHIRE W.	18·4	23·7	19·9	40·3	20·5

APPROVED SCHOOLS

District	Boys 8–13	Boys 14–17	Girls 8–13	Girls 14–17	Aggregate juvenile population 8–17
	High rate of application of treatment				
Cambridge	18·6	47·9	—	—	27·3
Oxford	15·7	29·4	18·2	20·0	21·9
Peterborough	22·0	17·1	—	12·5	18·2
Dewsbury	16·7	20·3	—	—	17·5
Wakefield	12·1	19·6	33·3	33·3	16·5
Bolton	13·5	19·8	22·2	20·0	16·3
Worcester	18·5	14·6	—	—	16·1
	Low rate of application of treatment				
CARMARTHENSHIRE	0·9	3·6	6·3	—	3·9
Wigan	3·4	4·2	—	—	3·5
SUFFOLK W.	6·3	1·5	—	16·7	3·8
WESTMORLAND	3·0	4·8	—	—	3·9

TABLE XVII. *Districts with High and Low Rates of Five Methods of Treatment (cont.)*

FINES

District	*Boys 8–13*	*Boys 14–17*	*Girls 8–13*	*Girls 14–17*	*Aggregate juvenile population 8–17*
		High rate of application of treatment			
Rotherham	55·0	59·0	42·9	15·4	53·6
Blackburn	41·0	46·7	27·8	60·0	42·8
Gateshead	40·5	37·7	45·0	31·6	39·3
S. Shields	37·7	31·6	16·7	28·6	35·2
Middlesbrough	31·4	37·3	48·8	23·9	33·7
Wolverhampton	34·8	36·6	15·1	14·3	33·6
Bootle	31·0	38·0	20·0	12·5	32·5
Grimsby	29·7	35·4	12·0	21·7	30·4
Sheffield	28·2	32·3	33·3	31·6	30·0
		Low rate of application of treatment			
LINCOLNSHIRE (Holl.)	—	1·1	—	—	0·4
CAMBRIDGESHIRE	—	3·1	—	—	1·2
Burnley	—	7·8	—	—	2·1
Portsmouth	0·8	5·9	2·8	—	2·4
CORNWALL	2·0	3·5	5·2	—	2·6
CAERNARVONSHIRE	3·2	6·3	—	—	3·7
Worcester	4·1	3·6	—	—	3·7
SUFFOLK W.	3·8	3·8	6·4	—	3·8
Reading	—	8·6	—	—	3·6
Newcastle	3·3	5·0	—	—	3·9
Southend	3·1	6·9	5·9	—	4·1

way of disposal equally for children and young persons of both sexes, but it can also be due to a preference for a measure with regard to one group of juvenile delinquents only. Likewise a low rate for a specific form of treatment may disguise the fact that there is still a considerable use of the measure for one group of offenders in the district besides an extremely rare

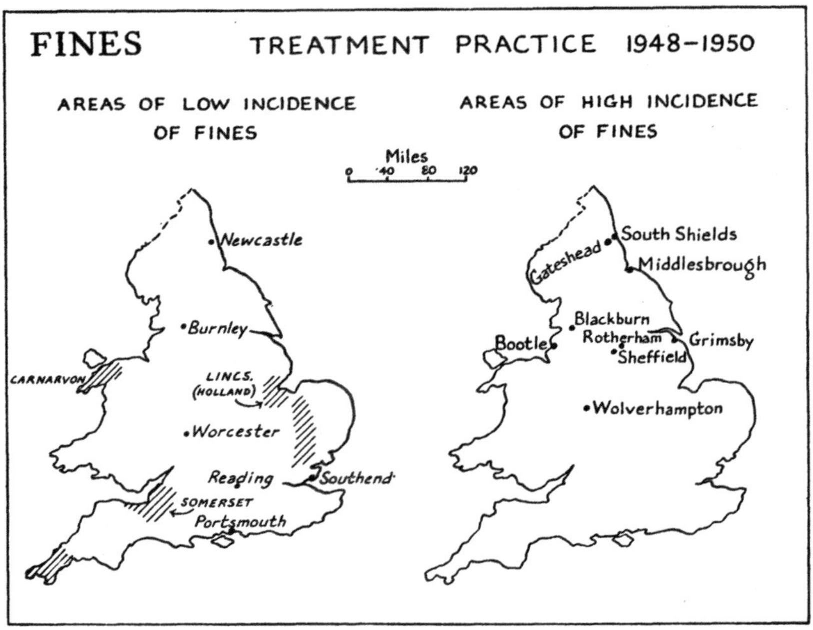

Map 3

application to those of other groups. For this reason in Table XVII the aggregate figures for all juvenile offenders have been supplemented by corresponding figures for children and young persons of each sex.

Variations in different sex and age groups are particularly significant with regard to discharge and fines. Among areas with a high rate of absolute discharge, Glamorgan favours this way of disposal in all four groups of juveniles, while Caernarvon and Burnley use it frequently only for senior boys (at a rate of 36·5 and 34·4 per cent. respectively compared with a district average for junior boys of 13·6), and the West Riding of Yorkshire for junior girls (45·4 compared with the district average for junior girls of 21·2). Likewise, conditional discharge is favoured for all four groups at Preston only, while Wigan and Worcester prefer it for junior boys (22·6 and 20·6 per cent. compared with an average of 11·3) and Tynemouth, Mid-Wales, and Doncaster for senior boys (26·8, 22·6, and 17·1 per cent. compared with an average of 9·6); at the same time, Wigan and mid-Wales do not apply conditional discharge to girls at all. At the other end of the scale, Cambridge remains below the district average of absolute discharge in all four age groups. Exeter, with its preference for absolute discharge, is, in all four groups, below the average for conditional discharge. With regard to fines, all districts with a high rate of this punishment use it frequently for more than one group; Blackburn, Gateshead, and Sheffield have exceedingly high fine-rates in all four groups. At the same time, in Cambridgeshire and Lincolnshire (parts of Holland) magistrates use fines sparingly in all four groups, and Burnley, Portsmouth, Worcester, Reading, and Newcastle in three of the four groups.

Police Cautioning

The criminological significance of a high and low rate of any treatment awarded by the court depends on the selection of cases which are prosecuted. Among the factors which determine this selection, none is more outstanding than the frequent or less frequent use of a non-judicial form of treatment, police cautioning. In the technical sense of the word, police cautioning means a procedure by which a juvenile offender is required to come to the police station to receive there in the presence of his parents a warning by a senior police officer. In rural districts with wide distances a police officer may call at the child's home and administer the warning there in the presence of the parents. If the officer on the beat stops any nuisance, he does not give a caution in the technical sense. While in Scotland[1] there has been a considerable discussion on the merits of police cautioning, this practice has had little publicity in England and Wales.

[1] L. H. Duncan, *Juvenile Delinquency in Ayrshire* (1944), pp. 23 and 69. *Police Warnings.* Report of the Scottish Advisory Council on the Treatment and Rehabilitation of Delinquents. H.M.S.O., Edinburgh, 1945. J. Ferguson, *The Young Delinquent in his Social Setting* (1952), pp. 5 et seq.

The practice of police cautioning has a bearing on criminal statistics. Since a discussion of the crime situation with regard to offenders of certain ages and sexes cannot be based on numbers of crimes known to the police, the alleged rise and fall of crime among certain groups of the population refers always to court figures. The actual amount of juvenile delinquency, however, includes those cases which never reach the courts because they are dealt with by police cautioning. Their number and proportion are by no means constant. Police cautioning has local variations and has fluctuations in the course of time. For any survey of the treatment practice of juvenile courts in certain districts, the practice of the local police must be taken into account.

The assessment of the merits or otherwise of police cautioning ought to be the subject of a special study. For the purpose of the present survey, however, it seemed sufficient to send letters to the Chief Constables of twenty-nine districts in which the courts made either an exceedingly high or an unusually low use of their powers to discharge juvenile offenders either absolutely or conditionally. In almost every case the response was most helpful. The discussion which follows is based on this information. Cautioning is regarded as an established function in the preventive work of the police. The selection of suitable cases is left to the discretion of superintendents or, in a small force, to the Chief Constable. As a rule cautions are administered for trifling cases, mostly non-indictable offences, of juveniles with no previous criminal record. It is, however, not uncommon to caution for simple stealing, and there are places where the number of cautions for indictable offences even exceeds the non-indictable cases. A police caution is also sometimes an expedient way of dealing with an offence committed by an absconder from an Approved School who, for educational reasons, should be returned at once to the school. Chief Constables in favour of cautioning assert that it has saved many hundreds of children from further steps into crime without the stigma of a court appearance. Others believe in the deterrent effect of such contact with the police which has been described as a stronger deterrent than an appearance before the court which is not followed by drastic action. Or else the practice is based on the common-sense experience that 'a word of advice and warning to a very young juvenile who has committed his first offence cannot be regarded as being amiss'. Sometimes the owner of stolen goods or damaged property wishes that the youthful sinner should not be brought before the court. Those who are sceptical about this method are in the minority. In an industrial town in the north Midlands police cautioning is regarded as being ineffective, and in a rural district in the north it was felt that it even diminishes the deterrent effect of subsequent court action. Before the court a juvenile who committed a fresh offence would technically be a first offender with a fair chance of being discharged, so that practically no action would be taken before the third offence. In some places police authorities seem to be anxious to avoid any appearance of an unequal handling of their prosecuting functions. Parents and neighbours are inclined to complain if one boy is prosecuted and another gets off with a mere police warning. In the last analysis, the issue involves one of the principal functions of the English juvenile court. There are two possible solutions to the problem. One is that the juvenile court should be the sole agency for dealing with any child or young person alleged to be in conflict with the law and with certain others in danger of becoming or remaining socially maladjusted. The other solution would be to institute a sifting process with an informal disposition of those cases which do not need the full weight of a decision by a court of law. With the English Acts of 1908 and 1933 the law-givers adopted the first solution with the result that, in spite of the practice of police cautioning, 28 per cent. of all juveniles before the courts are discharged. Comparative studies of legal institutions, especially of the American practice of settling cases by 'informal adjustment' outside the juvenile court, offer illustrations of the second solution. Any far-reaching proposals for similar methods in England must, however, take into account the strong tradition in English law that it is for the court to decide whether there is reasonable ground for a particular court action.

For the past J. H. Bagot, in the course of his studies on juvenile delinquency in Liverpool, investigated the fluctuations of police cautions and court proceedings in relation to the actual trend of juvenile delinquency in the years 1906–39.[1] The conditions in

[1] J. H. Bagot, *Juvenile Delinquency* (London, 1941), pp. 19–22.

Liverpool during this period allow some reflections on the way in which the discretionary power of the police affects the numbers of juvenile delinquents brought before the courts. In this particular case the divergent tendencies in the resort to police cautioning and prosecution are more apparent than any similarity of policy. From 1906 to 1911 the number of police cautions exceeded the court cases. Then a distinct increase in court cases coincided with a fall in police cautioning until in the First World War the practice was dropped altogether, just when juvenile delinquency had reached its peak. With the decline in delinquency after the war, police cautioning was resumed. Over the whole period of thirty-four years there was a negative correlation of −0·5 between police cautioning and court cases.

The material available for the present survey makes it possible, at least for two towns, to follow up for a number of years the figures for court cases and police cautions, both in respect of indictable offences. This makes it possible to assess the significance of these two methods in the light of the true amount of juvenile delinquency. The two towns are Great Yarmouth and Oldham, and the evidence illustrates two different situations. Fig. 2 indicates that in Great Yarmouth the curves for court proceedings and police cautioning run almost parallel save for a notable increase in the practice of police cautioning in 1951 at the expense of court proceedings. As far as the experience at Great Yarmouth is concerned, it is therefore fair to assume that the figures for court proceedings represent, though not the full amount of juvenile delinquency, at least its actual fluctuations throughout the years.

A comparison of these findings with the corresponding experience at Oldham reveals a somewhat different picture. On the one hand, Fig. 3 again illustrates the upward trend in delinquency reflected in a simultaneous rise in the number of police cautions and court proceedings. For the period under observation there is a positive correlation between these two functions of +0·54. There must, therefore, be parallel movements in some years and inverse movements in others. The rise in 1940 and in 1944 and the fall in 1942 apply to police cautions and court cases alike and thus represent true fluctuations in delinquency. At the same time, the rise in court cases in the fateful years of

1945 and 1948 seems at least partly to have been affected by a reduction in police cautions, and the fall in court cases in 1937, 1947, and 1951 is to a certain extent compensated by increasing numbers of police cautions, and vice versa.

These observations suggest that high delinquency rates based

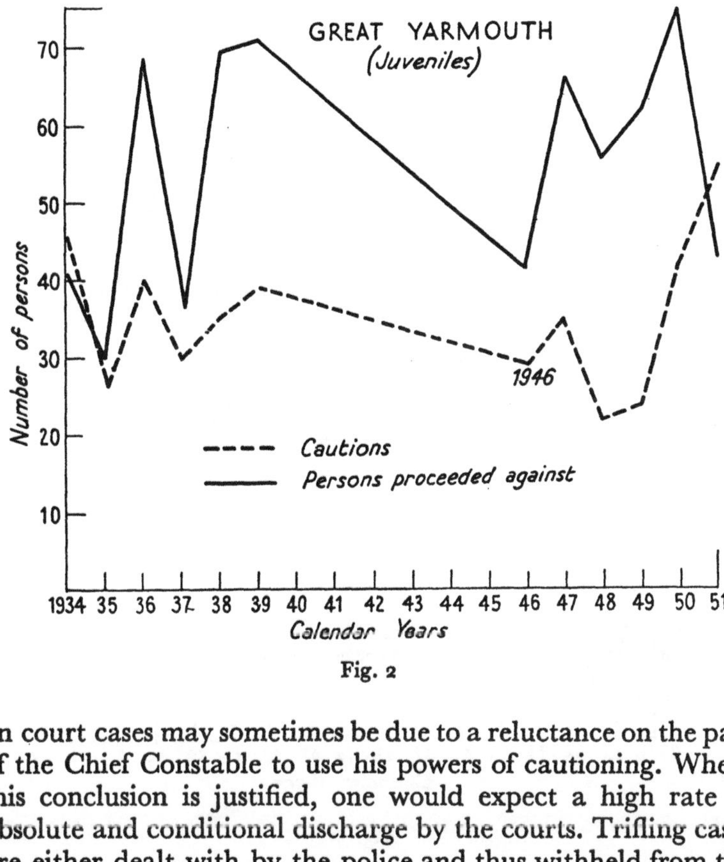

Fig. 2

on court cases may sometimes be due to a reluctance on the part of the Chief Constable to use his powers of cautioning. Where this conclusion is justified, one would expect a high rate of absolute and conditional discharge by the courts. Trifling cases are either dealt with by the police and thus withheld from the courts altogether, or brought before the magistrates where they inflate the court register and make a high proportion of discharges desirable if not inevitable.

Such conclusions from a chronological follow-up of the numbers of court cases and police cautions in individual districts are confirmed by an ecological comparison between conditions in different places. Table XVIII shows at the top three districts, Swansea, Glamorgan, and Merthyr Tydvil, with a small percentage of juvenile offences dealt with by police cautions and a high rate of offenders discharged by the courts,

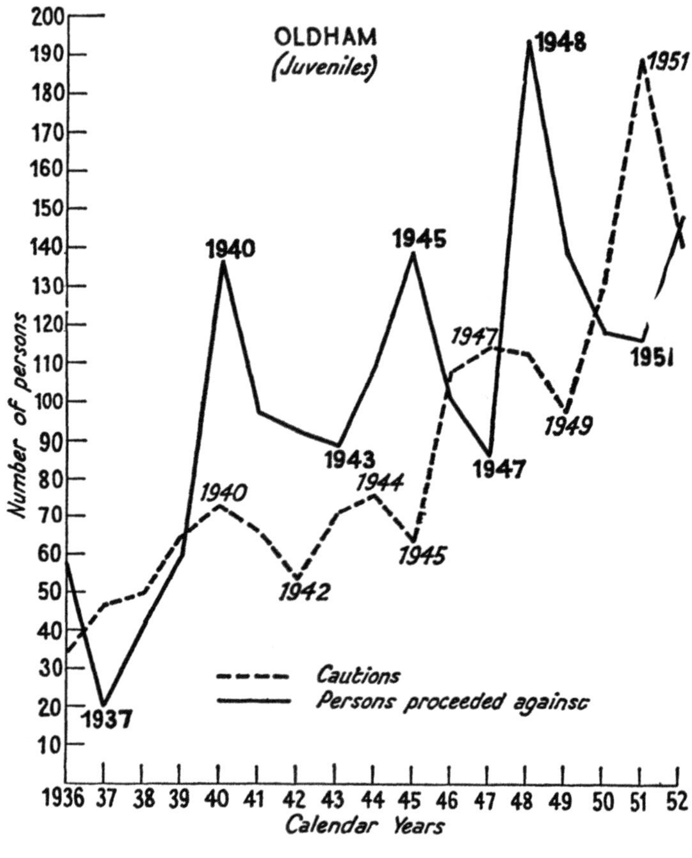

Fig. 3

and at the bottom two other districts, St. Helens and Cambridge, where the police make ample use of cautioning and only a negligible fraction of court cases ends with discharge. If further conclusions from this limited and provisional evidence are justified, the figures at Table XVIII seem to suggest that police cautioning is more frequently practised in small districts or in places with small numbers of delinquents.

TABLE XVIII. *Number of Court Cases, Police Cautions, and Discharge Rates in Selected Districts, 1948–50*

District	Court cases		Police cautions		Percentage of cautions related to court cases and cautions		Discharge rates for indictable offences
	Ind.	*Non-ind.*	*Ind.*	*Non-ind.*	*Ind.*	*Non-ind.*	*Ind.*
Swansea . . .	763	434	117	401	13·3	48·0	52·6
GLAMORGANSHIRE .	2,980	2,579	23	133	0·7	4·9	47·9
Merthyr Tydvil .	299	173	—	9	—	5·0	45·0
Bristol . . .	1,002*	1,110	96	93	8·7	7·7	37·2
Burnley . . .	257	61	94	65	26·7	50·0	32·2
Barrow-in-Furness .	275	247	64	78	18·9	24·0	31·6
St. Helens . .	483*	276	230	187	32·2	40·4	7·4
Cambridge . .	128	55	34	15	20·9	21·0	4·9

* These figures refer to the number found guilty; the number of court proceedings is not available.

Absolute and Conditional Discharge

The investigation of police cautioning throws some light on the significance of absolute and conditional discharge by the court within the prevailing system of measures for the treatment of juvenile offenders. If the full amount of police cautioning and other forms of abstaining from prosecution were known for every police district of the country, it would be possible to judge how far high discharge-rates are due to an inflated number of trivial cases brought before the court and where they indicate a deliberate or traditional policy of the magistrates. From the material available for the present survey, only a few tentative conclusions can be drawn. The West Riding of Yorkshire has a high delinquency-rate of 38·1 compared with a district average of 25·2 and a high rate of absolute discharge of 35·8 per cent. as compared with a district average of 17·2. Among the selected districts under observation the West Riding has a notably low rate of cautions for indictable offences. Subject to a further investigation of local delinquency which will be discussed in the next chapter, it is fair to assume that in this area many trifling offences are brought before the magistrates who dispose of them by absolute or conditional discharge. There is, at the same time, no district where magistrates discharge a high proportion out of a relatively small number of delinquents. This seems to suggest that the practice of discharge is, on the whole, not much determined by the magistrates' personal preference for this method. Burnley has still a fairly high discharge-rate in the face of what seems to be a frequently used practice of police cautioning. Whether this is due to local crime conditions or a typical attitude of the Bench cannot be decided from such data alone.

Within a system of corrective and coercive measures, absolute and conditional discharge have, as a rule, a negative function. In most of these cases nothing is done with, or in respect of, the offender who is discharged. The decision indicates that in the circumstances of the case it seemed to the magistrates advisable to abstain from any treatment proper whether constructive or punitive. In theory, there is a difference between the two statutory forms of discharge. An offender who is absolutely discharged leaves the court a free man, while a conditional discharge keeps him under threat of an impending court action for the original offence if he is guilty of any further wrongdoing. From a practical point of view, however, there is little to choose between these two forms of procedure. Even if an offender is tried who had been granted an absolute discharge some months before, this fact would be brought to the notice of the Bench. His relapse into criminal activities after a previous court appearance would then rightly influence the court in the selection of the treatment.

The negative character of absolute and conditional discharge applies to the legal function of the measures. From a comprehensive criminological point of view, a discharge may open the way for certain positive efforts. The deliberate abstention from intervening by legal action is sometimes used as an opportunity for bringing educative influences to bear on the offender. While for some magistrates to order a discharge is an expedient method of disposing of numerous trifling cases, others resort to this method only after they have brought home to the parents their share of responsibility and advised them on better ways of parental care and control, thus using these powers for something similar to an 'informal adjustment' at an American juvenile court.

The different motives which lead magistrates to a resort to absolute and conditional discharge give these decisions an ambiguous character. In a wider sense of the word, treatment includes discharge and for this reason the specific rates for the different treatment methods used so far in this chapter have taken into account the extent of absolute and conditional discharge in the same way as the use of probation, the committal to Approved Schools, or fines. If, however, one accepts a stricter conception of treatment and confines this term only to a procedure where something is done with, or required to be done by, the offender, absolute or conditional discharge is a renunciation of treatment rather than a form of treatment on its own. A survey of treatment practice must, therefore, supplement the study of the significance of all possible court decisions by an investigation of how magistrates dispose of those cases where they think that positive action should be taken. This means an investigation of court decisions apart from those resulting in absolute or conditional discharge.

The Alternative between Probation and Fines

The principal question before the magistrates, once they have decided that positive action is called for, is whether they should, in view of the young delinquent's needs and prospects, apply a constructive measure, or whether they should punish him. In the majority of cases this problem means an alternative between probation and fines. As has been mentioned before, the striking difference in the treatment practice of the pre-war years and the post-war period is a relative decrease in the use of probation and an increase in the resort to fines. This observation leads to the question whether the local distribution of treatment methods shows instances of high-probation areas with a low rate in the use of fines and vice versa, and thus provides sufficient evidence for the assumption that probation and fines are complementary. In the discussion which follows this question will be treated from a twofold angle. On the one hand, the relation between probation and fines will be studied within the wider framework of the main court decisions including absolute and conditional discharge; on the other hand, within the limited field of positive constructive and punitive measures alone.

If the observation is based on all five principal court decisions and on all juveniles of both sexes there is little evidence to support the proposition that the use of probation and fines is complementary. The treatment practice in Liverpool suggests an alternative use of probation and fines within certain limits. This high-delinquency area, though not included in the list of places with an unusually high rate of fines, is, with a rate of 29·3 per cent., still considerably above what could be regarded as a normal use of fines (14·0) and, at the same time, with a probation-rate of 29·1, below the normal application of probation (45·6). On the whole, however, the relation between the use of fines and probation in the treatment practice of the magistrates comes out more clearly if the investigation distinguishes between the usual four groups of juveniles. Rotherham is the only high-fine and low-probation area. There the magistrates fine 55 per cent. of the junior boys and 59 per cent. of the senior boys and put on probation only 12 and 13 per cent. respectively, as compared with a district average of 12·0 and 16·5 per cent. respectively for fines for junior and senior boys and 45·5 and 42·5 for probation. The treatment of girls offers more and better illustrations. In districts with small numbers of delinquent girls, magistrates prefer probation to fines, contrary to the general trend from probation to fines in the post-war years. Thirty-seven districts with a juvenile population of no more than 519,445 had only 963 delinquent girls in three years and none of them was fined. In thirty-two districts no junior girl was fined, and in fourteen other districts no senior girl was fined. At the same time, Cambridge and Eastbourne put all their delinquent girls on probation, and there were four other places where all junior and six where all senior girls were put on probation. All these districts had only small numbers of delinquent girls. Worcester had no more than four junior girls and Tynemouth four senior girls found guilty within three years and these small contingents were all dealt with by probation.

At the other end of the scale Blackburn, Gateshead, and Sheffield had exceedingly high rates of fines both for junior and senior girls. In five districts fines for junior girls were frequent, and five other districts had high fine-rates for senior girls. These thirteen districts had a juvenile population of

298,861 and 561 delinquent girls in three years, out of which 376 were in Liverpool. Prominent among districts with an abundant use of fines for junior girls alone are Middlesbrough and Rotherham with rates of more than 40 per cent. compared with the mean rate of fines for junior girls in all districts which was 8·5. Districts where only senior girls are frequently fined are headed by Wigan with a rate of 66·7 per cent. compared with the district mean of 10·6; they include Liverpool (40·2), known as a centre of delinquency, and Birkenhead (30·1).

In places with a considerable number of delinquents, a frequent use of fines keeps the rate of probation orders down. Blackburn, Gateshead, and Sheffield, with high rates of fines both for junior and senior girls, remain below the average rates of probation for girls of the same age group. Middlesbrough and Rotherham, with a frequent use of fines for junior girls, have probation-rates of 26·2 and 25 per cent. compared with the mean of 51·2. Magistrates in Wigan, Liverpool, and Birkenhead, which have high rates of fines for senior girls, put them on probation only at rates of 33·3, 30·4, and 36·5 per cent. respectively as compared with a mean of 57. These figures suggest that where a sufficient number of delinquents leave the magistrates a real choice in treatment policy, there is, with regard to girls, preference in some places for fines at the expense of probation, but, more frequently, a reluctance to fine girls and a preference for probation. Where numbers before the courts are very small, as often happens with girls, there is not much opportunity for a differentiated treatment practice. In Cardigan, out of 6 delinquent junior girls in three years, 2 were fined and 3 put on probation, and out of 7 senior girls at South Shields, 2 were fined and 5 put on probation.

A more characteristic picture of an alternative use of probation and fines emerges if one eliminates the hazardous factor of discharge and concentrates the investigation on the three statistically significant forms of treatment in the strict sense of the word, probation, Approved Schools, and fines. The computation of such specific treatment-rates for juvenile offenders of both sexes aged 8–17 years made it possible to sort out eight districts with high rates of fines and low rates of probation and four other districts with high rates of probation and low rates of fines. These two groups of districts are listed under A and B of Table XIX. A comparison of the two columns suggests that the difference in treatment practice is related to the size of the district and, even more, to the amount of delinquency in the area. The two districts with a juvenile population of more than 100,000 are among areas where courts use fines abundantly and probation sparingly, while the smallest area among

TABLE XIX. *Districts with a Complementary Use of Fines and Probation in the Treatment of Offenders who are not Discharged, 1948–50*

District	*Juvenile population*	*Total delinquency-rate*	*Rate of fines*	*Rate of probation*
England and Wales .	5,024,000	25·2	19·0	62·8
	A. *High fines and low probation*			
Blackburn . .	11,327	34·9	56·3	32·0
Gateshead . .	14,678	36·8	51·0	38·2
YORKSHIRE W. . .	188,550	38·1	47·7	41·5
Rotherham . .	10,563	31·3	72·5	18·6
Swansea . . .	18,496	36·9	45·0	31·4
Barrow . . .	8,105	32·3	42·5	32·9
Bootle . . .	10,440	61·8	45·3	32·0
Liverpool . .	108,050	55·0	39·7	39·5
	370,209			
	B. *High probation and low fines*			
Burnley . . .	8,630	27·7	3·1	85·8
LINCOLNSHIRE (Holl) .	12,580	20·7	0·6	82·0
SUFFOLK W. . .	12,902	12·4	4·7	88·0
MERIONETHSHIRE .	4,344	11·1	2·4	92·5
	38,456			

the twelve districts has few fines and the highest rate of probation. Seven per cent. of the juvenile population of England and Wales live in areas where the courts order fines frequently and probation rarely, and no more than 0·7 per cent. in high-probation and low-fine areas. If one goes back to local delinquency-rates which take into account those offences too for which the culprit was absolutely or conditionally discharged, differences between the two groups are revealed. Each of the low-fine and high-probation areas has a lower delinquency-rate than any of the high-fine and low-probation areas. All areas where a frequent resort to fines coincides with an infrequent use of probation have a delinquency-rate above the average for all districts, and three out of the eight districts have been classified as high-delinquency areas. At the same time, three out of the four areas with high probation-rates and low rates of fines have delinquency-rates below the mean and two of them are low-delinquency areas. This evidence confirms the personal view of an experienced Chief Constable that where magistrates are faced with smaller and more easily manageable numbers of juvenile delinquents, conditions are favourable for elaborate consideration of individual cases and thus for a frequent use of probation. In large and densely populated districts with a great amount of delinquency, magistrates have to dispose of a considerable number of young culprits before they are able to concentrate on cases which call for individual inquiries with a view to a possible probation order. Two of the eight high-fine and low-probation areas, the West Riding and Swansea, have an unusually high rate of cases discharged. Whether this means that in these places the high incidence of fines and the low rate of probation apply to delinquency cases with a true criminal substance, can only be decided in the light of local investigations which are to be discussed in the next chapter.

Changing Trends in Treatment Policy

The treatment practice observed by magistrates in any given period does not remain unaltered. In the course of time the amount and pattern of juvenile delinquency change. There is also a change in the types of cases brought to the notice of the magistrates and in their reaction to the needs and prospects of those they have to try. In order to assess the significance of the treatment practice of English juvenile courts, one has to analyse the post-war experience in the light of corresponding evidence from pre-war years. Table XX shows average treatment-rates for all districts for the pre-war period 1936–8 and the post-war years 1948–50. A comparison between the two sets of figures illustrates once more the increase in the use of fines at the apparent expense of probation. The decrease in cases where discharge was granted is insignificant, but within the group of cases discharged there is a shift from absolute to conditional discharge. A percentual decrease in probation at a time of rising delinquency does not necessarily mean a reduction in probation orders given and in the number of probationers under supervision. The annual average of juveniles put on probation rose from 13,864 in the years 1936–8 to 17,338 in the post-war years 1948–50.

TABLE XX. *Rates of Treatment applied by Juvenile Courts in dealing with Indictable Offenders: District Average*

	Absolute discharge	*Conditional discharge*	*Probation*	*Approved Schools*	*Fines*
1936–8	19·7	9·4	52·7	9·9	6·4
1948–50	17·2	10·9	45·6	9·4	14·0

Like pre-war and post-war delinquency, the trend of national figures for methods of treatment awarded by the courts covers a variety of parallel and diverging tendencies in the local field. The general spread of the changes indicated by average figures is illustrated by the frequency distribution of Table XXI. This table shows how the decrease in probation and the increase in fines has materialized in the various districts up and down the country. The number of districts using probation for 41–60 out of every 100 juvenile offenders remained constant, while the number of districts with a more generous application of probation declined from 34 to 11 and the number with probation-rates of less than 41 increased from 21 to 43. At the same time, the high number of 114 districts out of 129 where, before the war, no more than 10 per cent. of delinquent juveniles were fined, has been split up with the consequence that the number of districts with a more frequent resort to fines has increased.

From a criminological point of view, the question must be asked, what proportion of the juvenile population 'at risk' has been affected by the apparent change in the treatment practice of magistrates. Table XXII shows that before the war probation was applied to more than every second offender by magistrates who had jurisdiction over 41·2 per cent. of the juvenile population, while, after the war, only 23·7 per cent. of all juveniles

TABLE XXI. *Range of Application, by Numbers of Districts, of Absolute Discharge, Probation, and Fines in 1936–8 Compared with 1948–50*

Application of treatment per 100 offenders	Absolute discharge		Probation		Fines	
	1936–8	1948–50	1936–8	1948–50	1936–8	1948–50
	(number of districts)					
0–10	29	39	—	—	114	67
11–20	47	55	1	3	12	37
21–30	32	25	7	11	2	19
31–40	15	8	13	29	1	5
41–50	4	3	35	40	—	1
51–60	2	—	39	36	—	1
61–70	—	—	25	8	—	—
71–80	—	—	8	3	—	—
81–90	—	—	1	—	—	—
	129	130	129	130	129	130

TABLE XXII. *Range of Application per 1,000 of the Juvenile Population of Absolute Discharge, Probation, and Fines in 1936–8 and 1948–50*

Application of treatment per 100 offenders	Absolute discharge		Probation		Fines	
	1936–8	1948–50	1936–8	1948–50	1936–8	1948–50
	(juvenile population under jurisdiction, in thousands)					
0–10	563	733	—	—	5,253	2,701
11–20	2,350	1,965	23	217	409	1,323
21–30	2,276	1,908	216	544	121	901
31–40	479	356	248	828	17	78
41–50	95	62	2,005	2,093	—	11
51–60	37	—	2,387	1,192	—	10
61–70	—	—	768	123	—	—
71–80	—	—	141	27	—	—
81–90	—	—	12	—	—	—
	5,800	5,024	5,800	5,024	5,800	5,024

were under the jurisdiction of magistrates who use probation in this generous way. Before the war the overwhelming majority of juveniles, that is 90·5 per cent., were under the jurisdiction of magistrates who resorted to fines in no more than 10 per

TABLE XXIII. *Outstanding Differences between the Pre-war and Post-war Use of Fines*

	1936–8			*1948–50*			
District	*Juvenile population*	*Delinquency-rate per 1,000*	*Rate of fines*	*Juvenile population*	*Delinquency-rate per 1,000*	*Rate of fines*	*Difference*
Blackburn	16,160	22·1	19·5	11,327	34·9	**42·8**	+23·3
Middlesbrough	19,980	**48·2**	10·5	19,833	**55·0**	**33·7**	+23·2
Rotherham	10,930	12·0	8·4	10,563	31·3	**53·6**	+45·2
Grimsby	13,200	**23·0**	5·4	13,192	**55·0**	**30·3**	+24·9
Wolverhampton	20,751	13·1	5·1	19,698	30·1	**33·5**	+24·9
Sheffield	74,300	12·2	2·4	59,503	17·6	**30·0**	+27·6
Wakefield	8,430	16·5	—	7,040	17·2	23·1	+23·1
Rochdale	13,060	13·4	—	8,840	**40·7**	23·3	+23·3
	176,811			149,996			
Blackpool	17,980	15·3	18·5	12,671	32·8	5·5	−13·0
CAMBRIDGESHIRE	10,220	2·6	19·2	8,864	9·9	1·2	−18·0
Dudley	8,800	18·3	24·2	7,948	30·5	14·4	−9·8
	37,000			29,483			

Note: Areas of high delinquency and areas of high fines indicated by bold figures.

cent. of all cases, while after the war nearly one-half of this group had a higher probability of being fined once they had been found guilty of an indictable offence.

For the country as a whole, the changing trends in treatment policy can be described in this way. Magistrates with jurisdiction over a considerable part of the juvenile population resorted after the war more frequently to fines, while in respect of probation the largest of the groups of juveniles who were under the jurisdiction of magistrates with the same treatment practice had before the war a prospect of being put on probation in 55 out of 100 cases and after the war in only 45 cases.

For an assessment of the real importance of these figures,

the changing tendencies in court practice must be followed up within individual districts. While it is fair to assume that the majority of districts reflect the pattern as it is expressed in the difference between pre-war and post-war averages, it seems

TABLE XXIV. *Outstanding Differences between the Pre-war and Post-war use of Probation*

District	*1936–8* *Juvenile population*	*1936–8* *Delinquency-rate per 1,000*	*1936–8* *Rate of probation*	*1948–50* *Juvenile population*	*1948–50* *Delinquency-rate per 1,000*	*1948–50* *Rate of probation*	*Difference*
Rochdale	13,060	13·4	**79·5**	8,840	**40·7**	46·6	−32
Plymouth	30,250	12·2	**73·0**	23,415	19·5	46·3	−26
Wolverhampton	20,750	13·1	72·0	19,698	30·1	33·1	−38
NORTHUMBERLAND	58,500	16·0	70·4	50,945	30·6	32·5	−27·9
Tynemouth	9,510	13·1	68·3	8,307	**44·3**	36·6	−31·7
Newcastle	41,650	14·7	67·5	34,825	32·1	33·5	−34·0
Wigan	11,810	18·3	65·5	10,108	33·6	34·8	−30·7
MONMOUTHSHIRE	43,800	13·9	64·0	39,890	32·0	40·7	−23·3
YORKSHIRE E.	26,390	9·5	62·2	24,026	21·4	33·9	−28·3
Rotherham	10,930	12·0	54·2	10,563	31·3	14·8	−39·4
	266,650			230,617			
MERIONETHSHIRE	5,650	4·8	63·0	4,344	11·1	**79·2**	+16·2
SUFFOLK W.	14,780	8·0	56·3	12,902	12·4	70·0	+13·7
Isle of Ely	11,650	7·3	41·1	10,392	11·5	56·7	+15·6
Eastbourne	8,070	15·7	40·2	5,790	15·1	69·3	+29·1
Hull	49,500	20·7	37·8	41,640	**38·4**	48·3	+10·5
Warrington	11,180	12·9	32·6	9,746	36·3	51·1	+18·5
BERKSHIRE	32,500	9·0	32·2	33,417	17·5	57·3	+25·1
Stockport	19,280	13·8	29·2	15,566	**40·3**	42·6	+13·4
Northampton	13,820	11.9	27·3	11,536	23·6	51·0	+23·7
	166,480			145,333			

Note: Areas of high delinquency and areas of high probation indicated by bold figures.

desirable to study the non-typical cases, areas where a comparison between pre-war and post-war figures reveals a departure from the general trend. Tables XXIII and XXIV contain lists of districts where such deviations are shown. Compared with the general increase in the rate of fines by 7·6 for every 100 juveniles found guilty of indictable offences, there were eight districts with a juvenile population decreasing from 176,811 to 149,996 where the increase in the application of fines amounted to more than 23 for every 100 cases, and there were three other districts with a juvenile population decreasing from 37,000 to 29,483 where the percentage of fines had notably decreased. The districts with an unusually high increase in fines include two towns, Middlesbrough and Grimsby, which were high-delinquency areas both before and after the war. A third one, Rochdale, became a high-delinquency area after the war. The town with the highest increase in fines is Rotherham, where the use of probation decreased by 39·4 for every 100 juvenile offenders. Sheffield and Wakefield, too, with comparable economic conditions and a similar social structure, show a more than average increase in the number of fines. At the same time, Cambridgeshire has the greatest decrease in fines, accompanied by a growing resort to absolute discharge.

Three of the districts with a more than average increase in fines reappear in Table XXIV as areas with a more than usual decrease in the use of probation, Rochdale, Wolverhampton, and Rotherham. On the whole, ten districts with a juvenile population decreasing from 266,650 to 230,617 exceed the mean reduction in the percentage rate of probation, which is 7·1, by differences of more than 23. None of those ten places where magistrates restricted the use of probation was a high-delinquency area before the war, but two of them, Rochdale and Tynemouth, became so after the war. A marked fall in the percentage use of probation occurred in a north-eastern region comprising Northumberland, Newcastle, and Tynemouth. Plymouth and Rochdale are places where the decrease in the rate of probation occurred in districts which had been high-probation areas before the war. They are, even after the reduction in their probation-rates, still near to the mean. The nine districts where, contrary to the general trend, the use of probation increased, cover a larger juvenile population than the three localities with a decreasing application of fines. Only two of the nine districts where probation-rates increased from the pre-war to the post-war period became high-delinquency areas after the war, Hull and Stockport. None of the three districts where, contrary to the general trend, the use of fines decreased showed a rising proportion of probation orders.

The discussion of local differences in the proportion between probation orders and fines was based on two rates of figures: on an analysis of all court decisions on juveniles found guilty, including those who had been discharged; and on specific treatment-rates which refer to the relation between probation orders, Approved School orders, and fines, thus leaving apart absolute

TABLE XXV. *Districts with a Complementary Use of Fines and Probation in Cases which are not Discharged, 1936–8*

District	*Juvenile population*	*Total delinquency-rate*	*Rate of fines*	*Rate of probation*
England and Wales	5,800,000	14·3	8·4	73·2
	A. High fines and low probation			
CAMBRIDGESHIRE	10,220	2·6	23·5	57·2
Wallasey	13,460	23·2	21·5	50·2
Gateshead	16,720	30·2	42·4	42·9
Blackburn	16,160	22·1	34·8	48·8
Blackpool	17,980	15·3	24·4	57·1
Bootle	10,580	31·6	27·4	54·8
Liverpool	118,200	43·6	35·8	48·7
Warrington	11,180	12·9	22·5	52·3
Dudley	8,800	18·3	27·7	59·5
CARMARTHENSHIRE	24,650	12·7	30·0	60·0
Swansea	23,000	22·7	17·5	57·5
	270,980			
	B. Low fines and high probation			
Wigan	11,810	18·3	0·6	94·0
MERIONETHSHIRE	5,650	4·8	—	94·4
PEMBROKESHIRE	11,880	8·4	—	94·4
	29,340			

and conditional discharge where no treatment in the strict sense is called for. Such specific treatment-rates must also be used in order to show how far, in the course of time, a changing attitude on the part of magistrates towards probation and fines affected the treatment practice in different localities. The figures in Table XXV illustrate for the pre-war years 1936–8 the complementary use of probation and fines in the cases of offenders who were not discharged. There were at that time eleven areas with high rates of fines and low rates of probation. If one compares these pre-war figures with the corresponding data of Table XIX it becomes evident that five densely populated places, Blackburn, Gateshead, Bootle, Liverpool, and Swansea, were high-fine and low-probation areas both before and after the war, while the small county of Merioneth was a low-fine and high-probation area then and now. Cambridgeshire, Warrington, Dudley, and Carmarthen lost the characteristic coincidence of high fine-rates and low probation-rates, while Rotherham and Barrow showed this feature only in the post-war years. At the same time, Wigan and Pembroke no longer showed the disparity between unusually high probation-rates and almost no fines at all, while Burnley, Lincolnshire, and Suffolk became low-fine and high-probation areas in the post-war period. This is the evidence for consistent and changing policies in a complementary use of fines and probation. In terms of juveniles 'at risk', the changing trends in treatment practice had an adverse effect on the chances of being put on probation. Over a period when the total juvenile population of England and Wales decreased from 5,800,000 to 5,024,000, the number of juveniles under the jurisdiction of magistrates favouring fines and disfavouring probation increased by 36 per cent. from 270,980 to 370,209, and of those under jurisdiction of magistrates who held opposite views, preferring probation to fines, by 31 per cent. from only 29,340 to no more than 38,456.

Conclusions

In this chapter the question of uniformity or disparity in the treatment practice of magistrates has been approached from different angles. As a result, certain characteristic features of the ways in which English juvenile courts deal with offenders have become evident.

1. The general picture drawn from all districts of the country is that out of every 100 juveniles found guilty of indictable offences, magistrates put 45 on probation, discharge 17 absolutely, fine 14, discharge 11 conditionally, and commit 9 to Approved Schools. On the whole, magistrates favour probation for older girls (57 per cent.), absolute discharge for younger girls (21·2 per cent.), and Approved Schools for older boys (12·2 per cent.). If one leaves aside cases where the young

delinquent is discharged and concentrates on those where a constructive or punitive treatment in the strict sense of the word appears to be necessary, out of every 100 juvenile delinquents for whom such treatment is selected, 63 are put on probation, 13 committed to an Approved School, and 19 fined. Three out of every four juvenile offenders whose cases require more than an absolute or conditional discharge receive constructive treatment, either extra-mural or institutional.

2. These mean figures cover a considerable amount of conformity as well as a number of local variations in the treatment practice of the magistrates. Four-fifths of all juveniles in England and Wales live in areas where the treatment practice of the courts does not differ much from the average standard for all districts.

3. Within the range of marked deviation from the general standard there are, in respect of treatment methods apart from a mere discharge, five high-probation areas and nine low-probation areas, and twenty areas with high rates of fines and fourteen low-fine areas. A number of high-delinquency areas, Liverpool, Bootle, and the West Riding of Yorkshire, show a coincidence of low rates of probation and high rates of fines.

4. There is a certain amount of evidence for the complementary character of probation and fines. Beside other possible combinations, two characteristic patterns of treatment practice appear, either preference for probation coupled with a sparing use of fines, or sparing use of probation with ample resort to fines. An analysis of the distribution of all forms of court decisions for juvenile offenders of all ages and both sexes provides little illustration of such inverse relation between probation and fines. Such patterns come out more clearly for specific age groups of either sex. Rotherham has high rates of fines and low rates of probation for boys; Blackburn, Gateshead, and Sheffield have a general preference for fines, and put only few girls on probation. Where only few delinquent girls appear before the courts, magistrates very often refrain from fining them and put them on probation instead. If one leaves out all cases of discharge and analyses the relation between the three significant specific forms of treatment, probation, Approved Schools, and fines, one finds low probation-rates and frequent fines in eight districts, mostly large areas with high delinquency

rates covering 7 per cent. of the juvenile population of England and Wales, and high probation-rates combined with a sparing use of fines in four other localities, mostly small districts with low delinquency-rates covering no more than 0·7 per cent. of the juvenile population.

5. The outstanding feature in the changing trends of treatment practice between pre-war years and the post-war period is a shifting of the emphasis from probation to fines. Before the war, in seventy-three districts more than every second juvenile offender was put on probation; after the war this was done in forty-seven districts only. In pre-war days, in 114 districts no more than one in ten juvenile offenders was fined, but after the war such sparing use of fines prevailed in sixty-seven districts only. This development had the effect that the proportion of the juvenile population 'at risk' under the jurisdiction of magistrates with a notable preference for probation has been reduced from 41·2 to 23·7 per cent., while the proportion of those in districts where fines are given in more than 10 per cent. of all cases has been extended from 9·5 to 47 per cent.

6. The results of an analysis of the treatment practice of English juvenile courts before and after the war suggest a further question. Do high or low probation-rates and a sparing or frequent resort to fines indicate a different or a changing personal outlook on the part of magistrates, or do they reflect differences or changes in the pattern of delinquency among the rising numbers of juvenile offenders? This question cannot be answered by a mere reference to numbers of delinquents, but requires a qualitative investigation into the forms of criminal activities and the personal background of offenders at different places and periods. The next chapter contains certain qualitative observations on juvenile delinquency as a contribution to an adequate interpretation of local differences in the treatment practice of magistrates' courts in England and Wales.

CHAPTER IV

TREATMENT PRACTICE IN RELATION TO SPECIFIC FORMS OF DELINQUENCY

Different Forms of Delinquency

IN the foregoing chapters an attempt has been made to map out the topographical distribution of juvenile delinquency in England and Wales and to assess local variations in the treatment practice of English juvenile courts in the several police districts of the country. On the strength of the evidence produced so far the final question arises whether there is any relation between a characteristic treatment practice in certain courts, on the one hand, and the amount and specific patterns of delinquency, on the other. There are two possible answers to this question. It is possible that magistrates deliberately adapt their treatment practice to the amounts and forms of delinquency in their districts. At the same time it may be that the delinquency situation in a certain district has been affected by a characteristic treatment practice of the local magistrates.

A comparison between the incidence of juvenile delinquency and the way in which certain methods of treatment are applied by magistrates leads to correlations which are statistically significant with regard to three forms of treatment. For the years under observation, absolute discharge has a correlation to juvenile delinquency of +0·28, fines of +0·35, and probation of −0·25. These figures confirm in terms of statistics the observation made on several occasions during the preceding discussion that, where magistrates are confronted with great numbers of delinquents, they are inclined to dispose of a considerable proportion of them by the expedient means of discharge and fines, while, where they have only a moderate number of young offenders before them, they feel in a better position to consider individualized constructive treatment and thus to order probation. It would be wrong to say, on the strength of these statistical correlations alone, that a frequent use of probation has a favourable influence on the crime situation, and that the resort to absolute discharge and fines is accompanied, if not followed, by a high incidence of delinquency. Rather a tentative, negative statement can be justified by these figures. They show that the use of probation has not, as some of its critics maintain, any apparent undesirable effect on the extent of delinquency in areas where frequent probation orders are made. At the same time, the figures are a challenge to areas with a preference for absolute discharge and fines to re-examine the situation with a view to new experiments in treatment practice.

Statements like these are almost the last which can be made on the strength of a mainly quantitative analysis of the available evidence about juvenile delinquency. The situation confronting the Bench, no less than the conduct of boys and girls as it is affected by the way in which the courts handle the cases before them, is not only reflected in the number of those found guilty, but also in the typical patterns of their behaviour in general and the characteristic forms of their criminal activities in particular. The crime situation in the districts does not differ in rates of crime for the whole population or for certain age groups alone. It is determined also by the prevalence of serious or less serious offences, by the proportion between crimes of dishonesty, wilful damage, and sexual offences, or, within the large province of crimes of dishonesty, between breaking and entering, on the one hand, and simple stealing, on the other, or between stealing money or stealing food or toys. The high-delinquency area of Liverpool is not only characterized by consistently high delinquency rates, but also by more serious forms of lawlessness. While, for the country as a whole, 27·1 per cent. of all indictable offences committed by juveniles in the years 1948–50 were cases of breaking and entering, the corresponding figure for Liverpool was 38·3.[1] Even more important are the differences in respect of the personalities and past experience of the young offenders. This refers to the numerical relation, within different districts, between first offenders and repeaters, between school-children and wage-earners, and to the proportion, among local groups,

[1] Figures computed from *Criminal Statistics England and Wales 1948, 1949, 1950*, and (Liverpool) *Report on the Police Establishment and the State of Crime for the Year ending 31 December 1952* (1953).

of juveniles from poor homes, broken families, and with unsatisfactory personal relationships.

In order to interpret divergences in local treatment practice in the light of such qualitative assessment of juvenile delinquency in a locality, the statistical material used in the preceding part of the discussion had to be supplemented by field-work. For this purpose a total of 700 case histories from five selected districts was collected to provide qualitative data for a comprehensive assessment of the crime situation to which the local treatment practice, ascertained from statistical sources, applied.

Local Diagnosis of Five Selected Districts

Five districts were selected for field-work which could be expected to illustrate the work of juvenile courts under different conditions. Places were deliberately selected which had not previously been the subject of special criminological studies. The work began in Oxford City and was then carried to Oxford County with its predominantly rural character. The methods tested in these areas were further applied to two industrial places, Newcastle and Swansea. Finally, the work was extended to the West Riding of Yorkshire, a rural area penetrated by industry. In each of the first four of these districts, a sample group of 100 cases was collected from the Juvenile Court Register. For this purpose the following sampling method was used. The number of the required sample, that is to say, 100, was divided by the total number of delinquents for the three-year period. The proportion thus obtained, roughly one-half in the case of Oxford, and one-eleventh in the case of Newcastle, was taken as the fraction which had to be selected from each monthly intake of the courts. In order to neutralize seasonal variations, for 1948 the monthly figure was drawn from the first cases of the month, for 1949 from the middle cases, and for 1950 from the last cases. In the West Riding, with a contingent of 7,175 juvenile delinquents, a sample group of 300 cases was collected by a similar but somewhat simplified method. For the 700 cases all available information was collected from police authorities, probation officers, children's officers, education authorities, and other sources, and from this material case-studies were built up. In Oxford, Oxfordshire, Newcastle, and Swansea, the work was undertaken by the same field-worker.

Two others went to the West Riding. In Yorkshire it proved rather difficult to trace the past history of all relevant court cases. In the huge area of the West Riding there are forty-four petty sessional divisions, and there is a considerable amount of decentralization of the education authorities and the work of the Children's Officer. The boundaries of these administrative units do not correspond to the venue of the courts. The years chosen for this investigation, 1948–50, covered a period of transition, when a good deal of work in child care was transferred from education authorities to Children's Officers. This fact made it even more difficult to trace the relevant files. All these circumstances concurred to make the material from the West Riding less accessible, and therefore less uniform and comparable. If, in the end, all these difficulties were overcome, we owe this to the willing co-operation and the unfailing support which was generously given by the authorities and by numerous individual social workers and policemen. To all of them the author of this study remains deeply indebted.

In order to achieve the necessary uniformity, the assessment of the data in the case studies was in the hands of one research worker. The next step was to find out whether the collection of 700 case studies from five districts revealed any qualitative difference in the structure and characteristic forms of juvenile delinquency within these areas. The answer to this question required the help of elaborate statistical techniques. We were very fortunate in that facilities were granted under which this technical statistical work could be performed by the Social Survey. A coding system was arranged, twenty-one relevant criteria were transferred from the case histories to code sheets, and the latter handed over to the Social Survey. All facts and figures introduced in the discussion which follows are taken from tabulations worked out by the Social Survey. Throughout the whole course of this phase of the work, Mr. Leslie T. Wilkins, Senior Research Officer of the Social Survey, has stimulated these studies by his active interest and influenced their shape by his expert advice.

The data collected in the course of these investigations make it possible to characterize each of the five selected districts under observation by a 'local diagnosis'.[1] It is against this back-

[1] The figures given in the 'local diagnosis' of the five selected districts are com-

ground of social conditions in each particular locality that the results of any qualitative analysis of juvenile delinquency must be seen. As for the quantitative assessment of delinquency and rates of different forms of treatment, Table XXVI presents the figures obtained from the statistical investigations in the preceding chapters.

TABLE XXVI. *Details of Delinquency and Treatment Practice in English Juvenile Courts*

	Delinquency (Rate per 1,000)					*Treatment practice (Rate per 100)*				
	Boys 8–13	*Boys 14–17*	*Girls 8–13*	*Girls 14–17*	*All juveni*	*Absolute discharge*	*Conditional discharge*	*Probation*	*Approved Schools*	*Fines*
Oxford	27·2	51·0	3·0	5·7	19·7	5·1	3·2	39·0	21·8	24·6
Oxford County	24·8	42·1	1·1	3·4	16·3	19·6	14·4	43·7	11·0	7·6
Newcastle	53·8	72·5	1·6	7·4	32·1	44·5	9·3	33·5	8·2	3·8
Swansea	72·0	67·3	3·4	5·7	36·9	37·1	15·5	14·8	7·1	21·3
W. Riding	70·0	70·5	4·8	4·9	38·1	35·8	14·7	20·5	5·2	23·7
Industrial mean	55·9	64·7	4·7	6·5	32·3	14·9	10·9	42·1	8·8	18·8
Rural mean	19·2	32·8	1·8	4·9	13·2	13·1	12·2	49·2	10·2	8·7
Total district average	39·0	51·0	3·4	6·5	25·2	17·2	10·9	45·6	9·4	14·0
Standard deviation	24·5	18·9	2·2	2·5	11·7	9·6	6·8	16·8	5·8	9·7

The *City of Oxford* had 98,675 inhabitants according to the 1951 Census. Since the census was taken during the Easter vacation when undergraduates and pupils of boarding schools were not in residence, the Registrar-General's estimated figure for June 1951, which amounts to 106,400, is probably more in

puted from the following sources: *Census 1951, One Per Cent Sample Tables* (1952), Part I, page 83, Table II, 11, in connexion with *Classification of Occupations* (1950), p. iii; L. T. Wilkins, *Applied Statistics* (1952), No. 1, pp. 27–33; Registrar-General, *Statistical Review of England and Wales for the Years 1948, 1949, and 1950*, Part I, Medical, Table 16, p. 57 (1948), Table 16, p. 58 (1949), Table 26, p. 380 (1950); *Supplementary Statistics relating to Crime and Criminal Proceedings, 1950*; Institute of Municipal Treasurers and Accountants/Society of County Treasurers, *Police Force Statistics 1952/3*; Unpublished Home Office Statistics on Detection Rates; Institute of Municipal Treasurers and Accountants/Society of County Treasurers, *Children's Services Statistics 1952/3*.

line with actual conditions. Out of all males occupied or retired, only a very low rate of 26 per cent. are engaged in semi-skilled or unskilled occupations. The percentage of 31 for households where, in 1950, the chief wage-earner had a weekly income of at least £7. 10*s*. was comparatively high. Infant mortality was low, an annual average for 1948–50 of 23 per 1,000 live births. The rate of crimes known to the police per 1,000 of the population over 8 years rose from 9·3 in 1938 to 15·9 in 1950. There was a fairly normal police strength of one policeman per 657 of the population in 1953. Oxford police succeeded, in 1952, in clearing up 61 per cent. of crimes known to the police against 55 as an average for all police districts in England and Wales. Oxford had a comparatively high rate of children in care, 8·1 per 1,000 of population under 18 in 1952. Out of the total juvenile population of 10,933, in the three years under observation, 215 appeared before the juvenile court. This amounts to a delinquency-rate of 19·7 per 1,000. In all age groups the delinquency-rates in Oxford are of a medium size. They are below the industrial mean, but junior and senior boys have a higher delinquency-rate in Oxford than in rural districts. Oxford magistrates use absolute and conditional discharge very sparingly, but send every fifth juvenile offender to an Approved School.

Oxford County, an area of 748·8 square miles, has a population of 177,090 inhabitants. Thirty-two per cent. of the men, only slightly more than the national mean of 30, were occupied in semi-skilled or unskilled work. The rate of infant mortality, 24 per 1,000 live births, was almost the same as in Oxford City. The rate of crimes known to the police rose from 4·3 in 1938 to 9·8 in 1950. There was one policeman to 785 inhabitants, and the detection-rate was 50 per cent. The rate of children under the care of the County was 8·4 in 1952, which is high compared with the mean for all administrative counties of only 5·3.

Out of a juvenile population of 20,000, a number of 327 juvenile offenders appeared before the magistrates in the three-year observation period. This means a delinquency-rate of 16·3, notably below the district average of 25·2, though somewhat higher than the rural mean of 13·2. The delinquency-rate of boys between 14 and 17 years was 42·1 per 1,000. This comes nearer to the corresponding figure for Oxford City, which is 51·0, than to the delinquency-rate of their contemporaries in an aggregate of seven rural districts which was 32·8. The practice of Oxford county magistrates corresponds in the selection of each particular method of treatment to the policy of the country in general.

Newcastle, with 291,723 inhabitants, had only 27 per cent. of its occupied or retired male population engaged in semi-skilled or unskilled work and, correspondingly, a slightly more than average proportion of its households, 22 per cent., where the chief wage-earner brought in an income of £7. 10*s*. or more. At the same time infant mortality was 36 per 1,000 and thus somewhat above the national mean of 32. The rate of crimes known to the police was 7·1 in 1938 and 14·1 in 1950. Newcastle's police force is comparatively strong, amounting in 1952 to one policeman for 569 inhabitants, and the detection-rate of 55 is exactly the district average. The rate of children under care in 1952 was 6·5, thus corresponding to the average for all county boroughs which was 6·3.

Out of a juvenile population of 34,825, within three years 1,119 offenders appeared before the courts. The delinquency-rate for Newcastle was therefore 32·1. This crime situation has been very much the result of a high incidence of offences committed by senior boys. The delinquency-rate for boys of 14–17 years in Newcastle was 72·5. This exceeds the corresponding industrial mean of 64·7 by 7·8 and comes near to the 79·5 mark, beyond which a district would be classified as a high-delinquency area for senior boys. In Newcastle more than every second juvenile offender was discharged, the overwhelming majority of these, amounting to 44·5 per cent. of all offenders, were discharged absolutely. At the same time, magistrates made little use of fines; only 3·8 per cent. of all offenders were dealt with in this way.

Swansea had 160,832 inhabitants in 1951. One-third of the men occupied or retired belonged to semi-skilled or unskilled occupations. Correspondingly, the percentage of households where the chief wage-earner had a weekly income of at least £7. 10*s*. was slightly below the national mean, although still amounting to 16. The infant mortality rate was 38 per 1,000, thus slightly higher than at Newcastle and considerably above the rate for Oxford. The rate of crimes known to the police of 11·1 in 1950 was slightly below the national mean of 12. The police strength of one policeman for every 639 inhabitants was somewhat above the mean for all police authorities which was 674. The detection-rate of 46 was below the district average but still near to the national figure of 47·5 per cent. of all crimes reported.

In Swansea, out of a juvenile population of 18,996, within three years no less than 700 appeared before the courts. This means a delinquency-rate of 36·9 which exceeds both the national and the industrial mean and brings Swansea very near to the limit where it would be classified as a high-delinquency area. Contrary to the experience of magistrates at Newcastle, it is the junior boys who, with a delinquency-rate of 72 per 1,000, swell the ranks of juvenile offenders at Swansea. Like the Newcastle magistrates, the juvenile court in Swansea discharged every second young law-breaker. There was a slightly higher incidence of conditional discharge, amounting to 15·5 per cent. of all court orders. At the same time, Swansea is a low-probation area. Only 14·8 per cent. of all juvenile delinquents were put on probation.

The West Riding of Yorkshire is an area of 2,780 square miles. In 1951 the whole county had a population of 3,480,066 inhabitants. Out of these, 1,891,290 lived in ten large towns which are county boroughs with their own police forces, while the rest of the 1,588,776 inhabitants belonged to the administrative county and were under the jurisdiction of the West Riding Constabulary. Map 4 gives an impression of the size and social structure of the district. Six of the big industrial towns form a close neighbourhood in the southern centre of the county, but between their boundaries the county with its constabulary covers stretches of mixed rural and industrial development interspersed with small towns such as Morley and Ossett, and, on the fringes of this industrial area, a number of residential districts of a rural character with smaller industrial centres. Outside this conurbation there is rural countryside. In the south-east corner, however, four towns are carved out within and around the adjacent boroughs of Sheffield and Rotherham. As in Swansea the percentage of men occupied in semi-skilled and unskilled work (34) and the rate of infant mortality (38) were somewhat above the national mean. The rate of crimes known to the police had risen above the national mean. It was 5·7 in 1938 and 13·7 in 1950. The strength of the constabulary,

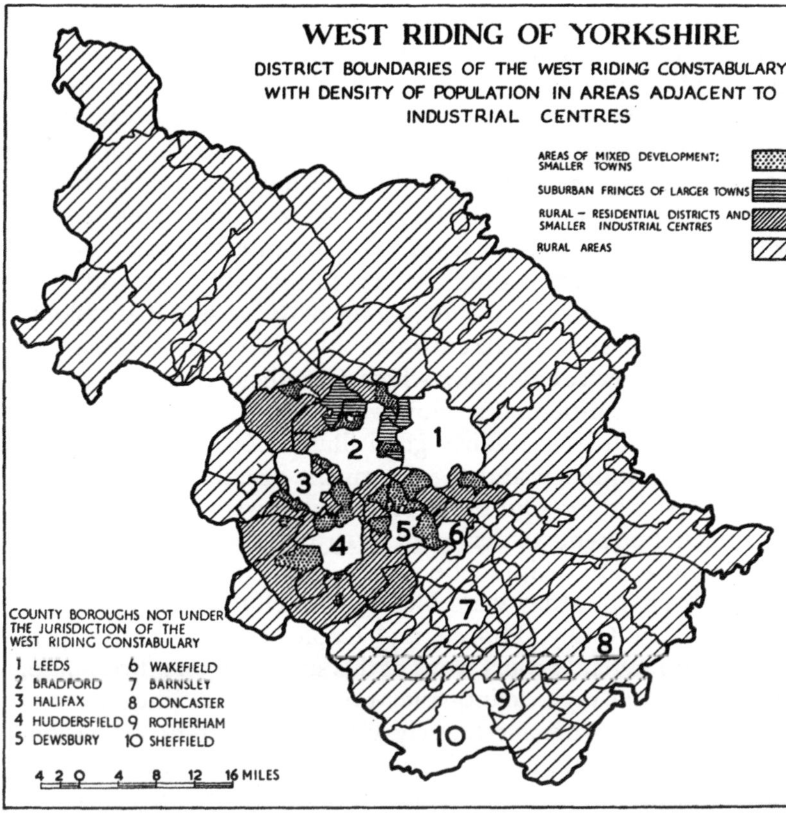

Map 4

with one policeman for every 730 inhabitants, was, as in most other counties, below the national mean. The detection-rate of 48 corresponded to the national mean, though it was still somewhat below the district average. The rate of children in care remained, at 4·4, below the county mean of 5·3.

Out of a total juvenile population of 188,550 in the West Riding, 7,175 appeared before the courts in three years. The

West Riding, with a delinquency-rate of 38·1, is a high-delinquency area. In the field of juvenile delinquency the West Riding figures exceed the national mean in a more marked way than in the crime situation in general as it is indicated in the rates of crimes known to the police. Compared with industrial districts in Lancashire and Staffordshire, the West Riding figures for delinquent girls are below normal, but they exceed those industrial delinquency-rates both for junior and senior boys with rates of 70 and 70·5 respectively. Again, the West Riding as a whole can be classified as a high-discharge and a low-probation area, although the rate for absolute discharge (35·8) is slightly lower and the rate for probation (20·5) somewhat higher than in Swansea. For an interpretation of the figures for the West Riding one has to take into account that this is an area served by forty-four petty sessional divisions. Delinquency- and treatment-rates for the whole district are based on numerical averages which may themselves cover considerable local differences. However, even with this qualification, the results give a fairly good illustration of the extent of juvenile delinquency and the treatment practice of the courts in the West Riding. Out of the eight courts with forty and more juvenile delinquents to deal with in 1950, seven had the characteristic pattern of a high delinquency-rate and a relatively high rate of discharge; they were Batley, Castleford, Keighley Boro, Morley Boro, Otley, Thorne, and Goole. Within the group of courts with juvenile court work of this size, only one, Brighouse, responded to a high delinquency-rate not with a liberal use of discharge, but with a relatively frequent resort to probation. With this treatment policy it corresponds to the practice of the two adjacent boroughs of Halifax and Huddersfield which are high-probation areas.

Patterns of Delinquency

An analysis of a selected number of criminological and social data shows that, in certain aspects, the groups of juveniles before the courts in all, or at least in three or four out of the five districts, consist of the same types of delinquents. Besides this relative conformity, there are several local peculiarities in the distribution of characteristics among delinquents before the courts in individual districts. For technical reasons a limitation of the material used for statistical calculation was inevitable. Out of the total of some 700 case histories, a small number did not yield sufficient information and had to be discarded. Likewise the total of sixty-five girls in the five sample groups was too small to allow the division of the total into the two sexes. The calculations which follow and the conclusions drawn from them refer, therefore, to 612 boys, or, in respect of specific criteria, to those boys out of this total for whom relevant information was available.

TABLE XXVII. *Percentages of Certain Criminological and Social Factors in Five Selected Districts*

	Oxford	*Oxford County*	*Newcastle*	*Swansea*	*W. Riding*
Wage-earners .	27	22	18	12	22
Simple stealing .	58	74	48	72	54
Repeaters . .	27	26	49	43	43
Low intelligence .	33	31	21	20	44
Weak or aggressive characters .	73	73	76	64	82
Broken homes .	36	18	30	13	31
Family disharmony	12	8	10	9	12
Lack of discipline .	27	26	25	35	25
Crime by other members of the family . .	30	17	15	27	19

Table XXVII illustrates the common characteristics and the local variations in respect of selected single factors for boys before the juvenile courts. In all five districts there were unsatisfactory relationships in the families of 8–12 per cent. of the boys. In all the districts, with the exception of higher figures for Swansea, there was a lack of home discipline in the families of 25–27 per cent. of the boys. In three districts, approximately every second boy before the court was guilty of simple stealing, but in Oxford County and in Swansea three out of four committed this offence. In three districts 43–49 per cent. of the boys had appeared in court before, but in Oxford City and County only slightly more than one in every four boys were repeaters. Again in three districts, 15–19 per cent. of the boys came from families where at least one other member was involved in crime, while in Swansea and Oxford City the proportion of such cases was higher. In the incidence of broken homes, the proportion of wage-earners and the distribution of intelligence and character traits among the boys, local differences were more striking. There were only 13 per cent. of boys before the juvenile court in Swansea who came from broken homes, while in Oxford there were more than one out of three. There were only few wage-earners in Swansea compared with more than one out of four boys before the juvenile court in Oxford. Swansea and Newcastle had few but the West Riding many boys described in school reports as of low intelligence, and again Swansea had a moderate and West Riding a high proportion of boys who had a record of undesirable character traits.

For an interpretation of these figures one has to bear in mind that they illustrate the situation presented to the magistrates by social reports submitted to them, and that these data are not a reliable basis for a comprehensive picture of the forms and amount of virtual delinquency in these districts. A predominance of certain unfavourable personal factors among the court cases of a particular place may be due to one of two reasons. It may be a reflection of circumstances which are widespread among the young generation in that locality and will therefore be found also among those juveniles who appear before the courts. It may, however, also be the effect of a negative selection when ordinary boys from normal families keep clear of unwelcome contacts with the law, and court cases are mainly recruited from difficult boys and problem families. The figures in Table XXVII give the impression that in Oxford, on the whole, the court had to deal with a selection of more serious cases. There were older boys, boys from broken homes or from families where other members too had criminal experience, although there was at the same time only a relatively small proportion of repeaters. Swansea gives the impression of a place where a large number of ordinary boys appeared before the court, younger boys of good intelligence, often from complete families, and engaged in simple stealing. It is an open question whether the high rate of boys from families with a lack of discipline is, at least partly, an indication of strict local standards of assessment rather than of conditions which are worse than elsewhere. The considerable amount of other forms of lawlessness in the family lends some colour to alleged unsatisfactory home discipline, unless the evidence is again affected by a more rigid code which brands a wide range of violations of the law as criminal offences.

These last observations suggest that a calculation of the frequency of selected single factors among boys before juvenile courts can do no more than provide a first preliminary orientation. Modern criminological research has shown conclusively that an analysis of simple characteristics of offenders alone never leads to a satisfactory explanation of crime and its causes. Likewise the selection of the appropriate treatment by magistrates is very rarely determined by the prevalence of one or the other personal or social factor. The decision of the court requires a comprehensive view. A young delinquent and his life are characterized by a composite pattern of personal circumstances and social conditions. Rates for single factors alone, however, leave open the question how far various criminological and social data apply to different boys or are typical of the same boys. Is it characteristic of boys before Oxford County magistrates that they are repeaters engaged in simple stealing, or are those who are charged with simple stealing just the first-offenders? Does the comparatively small number of repeaters in Oxford come from the numerous broken homes? In order to make the evidence more conclusive, rates of single factors must be supplemented by rates for configurations of several factors.

A number of combinations of two factors are presented in Table XXVIII. The figures suggest that the type of older boy with a previous court appearance has a similar share in the court cases of all five districts. Repeaters between 13 and 17 years of age seem to contribute something like one-fifth to one-quarter of the total juvenile court cases, with Oxford County somewhat below and the West Riding slightly above this rate. The same pattern, though with less marked differences, is characteristic of young wage-earners with previous convictions. The figures in Table XXVIII confirm the impression that in Oxford the boys before the court are in more than every fourth case older boys from broken homes. The proportion of Oxford boys from broken homes where other members of the family are involved in crime is greater than in any other of the five districts. However, those older boys in Oxford of whom many have a bad background frequently content themselves with simple stealing. In this they seem to resemble their contemporaries in Swansea where the figures point to unfavourable endowment rather than to adverse home conditions. In the West Riding, too, a slightly marked prevalence of the hard core of older repeaters seems to

TABLE XXVIII. *Percentages of Configurations of Two Criminological and Social Factors among Juvenile Delinquents in Five Selected Districts*

	Oxford	*Oxford County*	*Newcastle*	*Swansea*	*W. Riding*
Higher age group and repeaters .	20	17	26	25	27
Wage-earners and repeaters . .	9	5	8	7	12
Higher age group and broken home	27	12	15	5	18
Repeater and broken home . .	11	6	15	3	12
Broken home and family crime .	17	6	8	4	5
Simple stealing and higher age group	38	47	18	38	29
Simple stealing and repeaters . .	17	18	28	28	26
Low intelligence and weak or aggressive character . .	32	31	20	17	43

be attributable to personal factors rather than to home conditions. Oxford County, representing a rural district among the areas under observation, shows the least harmful picture. Oxfordshire has only a small contingent of the hard core of older repeaters and a high proportion of older boys engaged in simple stealing only. In Newcastle the magistrates have before them a group of juvenile delinquents who seem to correspond in most respects to what may be regarded as typical of boys before a juvenile court in England and Wales. Almost all the figures given for Newcastle are similar to what the majority of other districts have in common. One out of every four boys is a repeater between 13 and 17 years of age; 15 per cent. of the boys are repeaters from broken homes, although fewer of the older boys than in Swansea are content with simple stealing.

Such are some conclusions which can be drawn from the percentage figures for a number of two-factor combinations. As long as they are only used to illustrate the situation with which a particular court is confronted, it is irrelevant whether these combinations correspond to what could be expected from the mere fact of the numerical relation of the underlying single factors, or whether there are certain specific combinations of factors beyond the range of statistical expectation. However, if, at the same time, they are used to throw some light on the characteristic forms of local delinquency, the question must be asked whether there are any configurations more frequently represented than expected and therefore indicative of the particular pattern and the social conditions of local delinquency. Out of the figures in Table XXVIII the high proportion of older boys guilty of simple stealing in Oxford, Oxfordshire, and Swansea is what one has to expect in view of the numerous boys of 13 and over and of the many charges of simple theft. At the same time, the unfortunate coincidence of low intelligence with undesirable character traits reflects not only the frequency of either low intelligence or undesirable traits, but is beyond this, as a combination in itself, typical of the court cases in certain districts. According to the frequency of these two criteria, out of every 100 boys before the courts one had to expect 13 in Swansea, 24 in Oxford, and 36 in the West Riding to show *both* low intelligence *and* undesirable character traits, while actually the combinations occurred among 17, 32, and 43, out of every 100 boys respectively. The same applies to the prevalence of crime among members of a broken family. While ten of such cases would be expected in Oxford, actually 17 out of 100 boys had this situation as their background. It is therefore fair to assume that in three of the districts an interaction of low intelligence and unfavourable character, and, in Oxford, social maladjustment in a broken home are specific characteristics of delinquency in these localities.

For a description of the types of juveniles before the courts in each of the five districts, one can go one step farther beyond a mere summing up of coinciding factors. For a comprehensive view, personality and social background are composite concepts which allow a certain variation in the individual criteria which in their sum total characterize a boy and his environment. Whether a boy's home is a good or a bad one depends on whether he lives in a complete natural family or comes from a broken home, whether there are, or are not, satisfactory personal relationships in the family, whether there is, or is not, proper discipline, and whether he alone among members of the family, or any other member as well, has been concerned in criminal activities. A

TABLE XXIX. *Home Conditions of 573 Boys before the Courts of Five Districts, grouped on a Four-point Assessment*

	Oxford		*Oxford County*		*Newcastle*		*Swansea*		*W. Riding*	
	No.	%	No.	%	No.	%	No.	%	No.	%
Good homes 4 or 3 good points	60	*70*	63	*78*	73	*80*	72	*75*	73	*80*
Fair homes 2 good, 2 bad points . .	14	*16*	11	*14*	14	*16*	18	*20*	37	*15*
Bad homes 4 or 3 bad points.	12	*14*	6	*8*	4	*4*	5	*5*	11	*5*

family to which, in at least three out of these four criteria, a positive score could be given would be regarded as a good or satisfactory home, and a family with at least three unsatisfactory criteria as a bad home, while those which scored two on either side would be classified as fair. From the evidence available there was sufficient information for the home conditions of 573 boys. Table XXIX shows to what extent boys in the five districts came from a good and satisfactory home or from bad homes. The impression prevails that in all districts a high proportion of 70 to 80 per cent. of the boys came from good or satisfactory homes. The lower margin of 70 applies to Oxford with a comparatively high rate of boys from bad homes. However, even the home background alone is not always the decisive factor for an explanation of the boy's delinquent behaviour and for the selection of an appropriate treatment by the magistrates. The deeper roots of the more serious forms of social maladjustment must often be sought in a coincidence of personal factors and social conditions. In order to take into account the interplay of such personal and social factors, 568 of the boys were further grouped in a different way. In addition to the four home factors, one further positive or negative mark was given for absence or prevalence of a history of maladjustment as a characteristic symptom of delinquency. It was assumed that boys with at least four positive scores in respect of these five criteria had a good personal background while boys with at least three negative scores were classified as boys with a bad personal background, with an intermediate classification as fair for those who scored three positive and two negative marks. Table XXX shows the

TABLE XXX. *Personal Background of 568 Boys before the Courts of Five Districts, grouped on a Five-point Assessment*

	Oxford		*Oxford County*		*Newcastle*		*Swansea*		*W. Riding*	
	No.	%	No.	%	No.	%	No.	%	No.	%
5 or 4 good factors.	54	*63*	61	*77*	72	*80*	71	*74*	166	*75*
3 good, 2 bad factors	15	*18*	11	*14*	13	*15*	18	*20*	36	*17*
5, 4, or 3 bad factors	16	*19*	7	*9*	5	*5*	6	*6*	17	*8*

result of this grouping. It gives a slightly different picture only compared with the distribution of boys with good or bad home background. Once more Oxford, with a rate of nearly one in five, has the highest proportion of boys seriously affected by a coincidence of crime-promoting factors. At the same time, the distribution of boys with a good personal background among court cases in the five districts is less evenly spread than that of boys from good homes.

There appears to be a somewhat greater difference between the five districts if a further element is taken into account, and high or low intelligence is added to the configuration of four home factors and the history of maladjustment. Table XXXI shows the results of this six-point assessment. It was assumed that boys with at least four positive scores in respect of the six criteria were 'good boys', while boys with at least four negative scores were 'bad boys'. This working hypothesis of a six-point assessment of 'good' or 'bad' boys is based on the further assumption that adverse personal characteristics make bad home conditions even worse, while good personal factors may balance adverse home conditions. With this qualification, it appears that Oxford still exceeds the four other districts in the proportion of 'bad boys' before the court, but the proportion of these difficult cases is smaller than the rate of boys who have only a bad home or personal background. A similar observation applies to Newcastle and Swansea. There are more boys from bad homes than those who are assessed as 'bad boys' on a comprehensive assessment of home conditions and personal factors.

As in the preceding observations of this section, the factors under discussion are primarily intended to describe the position of magistrates in each of the five districts. If the figures for

TABLE XXXI. *Home Conditions and Personal Factors of 571 Boys appearing before the Courts of Five Districts, grouped on a Six-point Assessment*

	Oxford		*Oxford County*		*Newcastle*		*Swansea*		*W. Riding*	
	No.	%	No.	%	No.	%	No.	%	No.	%
6, 5, or 4 good factors . . .	53	*62*	55	*66*	75	*83*	76	*80*	152	*69*
3 good, 3 bad factors	23	*27*	23	*28*	13	*14*	16	*17*	58	*26*
6, 5, or 4 bad factors	9	*11*	4	*6*	2	*3*	3	*3*	9	*5*

Oxford reveal a comparatively high proportion of delinquents from bad homes and, on the strength of that assessment, of 'bad boys', this means that, for one reason or another, this is the situation with which the juvenile court in Oxford is confronted. The treatment practice of the magistrates must be seen in this light. The question arises whether a high proportion of delinquents from bad homes means that there are many Oxford boys, and thus many delinquents, who live in bad homes, or whether, in Oxford, ordinary boys from good homes do seldom appear before the court. A conclusive answer to this could only be found by an extension of the investigation into the personal circumstances and social background of non-delinquents. Short of this, the experience of evacuation, when children from East London shared the homes of their Oxford contemporaries, lends substance to the assumption that it is the smaller number of delinquents from good homes rather than the existence of a widespread group of problem families which explains the situation before the Oxford juvenile court. London children billeted with Oxford families of the same or a similar occupational status as their parents often found the mode of living differing from the one to which they were accustomed, and not always to their liking. There was, for example, an insistence on table manners, there were early bed-times, and foster-mothers seemed more strict than the mothers at home in what they regarded as respectable in the relations between boys and girls.[1] If this experience can be generalized it would mean that a large stratum of the population of Oxford keeps to a standard of living which makes it less probable that ordinary boys from normal families are charged with offences before the court. The high proportion of households where the main bread-winner has a weekly income of at least £7. 10*s.* fits in well with this picture, and the moderate rate of juvenile delinquency, especially of the younger age group, is further corroborating evidence. If this interpretation is correct, the unusually high percentage of boys from bad homes or with personal difficulties is not a reflection of poor social conditions in Oxford, but rather the result of a negative selection of boys who have to appear before the court.

In the light of these observations on court cases in Oxford, the figures for Newcastle and Swansea seem to indicate a different picture. In both places at least four out of five boys before the court, an unusually high proportion, have been classified as 'good boys'. Especially in Swansea the evidence suggests that it is very much the ordinary boy from a complete family with good personal relationships charged with simple stealing who fills the ranks of young offenders before the juvenile court.

On the strength of this evidence, the situation which confronts the magistrates in the five districts under observation can be described in more detail. In all districts, nearly one-fifth to one-quarter of the male offenders before the juvenile court were boys between 13 and 17 years who had been before the court before. Between 8 and 12 per cent. of all boys came from families with unsatisfactory personal relationships.

In *Oxford*, with a moderate delinquency-rate for junior boys and a delinquency-rate for senior boys which is exactly the district average, as many as 27 per cent. of the delinquents were wage-earners, and a considerable number had an unfavourable

[1] *London Children in Wartime Oxford*, by a Barnett House Study Group (1947), pp. 22 and 34.

home background; among 100 boys before the court, 27 were 13 years and over and came from a broken home, and 14—at least twice the number in the other four districts—came from families which, according to usual standards, were classified as bad homes. At the same time, 38 per cent. of all cases were older boys content to engage in simple stealing, and only 9 out of 100 boys were wage-earners with a previous court appearance. It was apparently the comparatively small hard core of older repeaters who committed more serious offences than just simple stealing.

In *Oxford County*, with delinquency-rates for boys somewhat above the rural mean, there is no evidence of outstanding features in the boys' social conditions. Out of 100 boys, 74 were charged with simple stealing, among them 47 older boys between 13 and 17 years of age. Only 5 per cent. were wage-earners with a previous court appearance.

In *Newcastle* the delinquency-rate of senior boys exceeded the industrial mean. Nearly every second boy before the court was a repeater. Among every 100 boys before the court, 49 had a previous court appearance. Out of these, 23 belonged to the age group 8–12 years, and 26 were between 13 and 17 years; 41 were school-children and only 8 wage-earners. At the same time, more than every second case was an offence other than simple stealing. This means a high incidence of breaking and entering with only a few single cases of wilful damage. In this context may be added a comment by the field-worker who observed that the wharves of Newcastle were much more accessible to unauthorized persons than the docks at Swansea. Otherwise there is no statistical evidence of outstanding social and criminological circumstances. On the whole, the boys' personal circumstances and social conditions corresponded to the typical picture of juvenile court cases. Eighty per cent. of the boys came from what has been classified as good or satisfactory homes. Only every fifth boy showed low intelligence plus undesirable character traits. If one reads the case studies from Newcastle one has the impression that many of the delinquent boys came from poor homes, although Newcastle had a fairly high percentage of twenty-two households with the main bread-winner earning at least £7. 10*s*. a week. One also has the impression that while the incidence of broken homes among court cases amounted to what is almost a standard percentage of 30, more frequently than in other places was the disruption due to the death of a parent rather than to a breaking of the family ties.

In *Swansea*, where the delinquency-rate for junior boys markedly exceeded the industrial mean, juvenile delinquency as reflected in court cases showed characteristic patterns. The picture was dominated by young boys, normal boys from stable families who were engaged mostly in simple stealing. Eighty-eight out of 100 boys before the court were schoolboys, only 17 per cent. had low intelligence plus undesirable character traits, and only 13 came from broken homes. The forms of delinquency resemble those of rural Oxfordshire, in that almost three out of every four boys were charged with simple stealing.

In the *West Riding of Yorkshire*, junior boys and, to a lesser degree, senior boys exceeded the industrial mean in their delinquency-rates. In an unusually high number of cases, 43 out of 100, the boys were described to the magistrates as of low intelligence plus undesirable character traits. Slightly more than every second boy was charged with simple stealing, somewhat less than every second was a repeater, a picture which corresponds to the experience in other places. However, the percentages of twenty-seven older repeaters and of twelve wage-earners with a previous court appearance were higher than the corresponding figures for any of the other four districts under observation. The statistical evidence suggests that there is the usual high proportion, eighty boys, coming from families which, from a psychological point of view, were classified as good or satisfactory homes. At the same time, the case studies reveal apparent symptoms of poverty among the families of the young delinquents. Families were large. There seemed to be a good deal of overcrowding.

It is in the light of these characteristics of the local delinquency situation as it appears to the Bench, that the treatment practice in the individual district must be seen. In Oxford, with older boys before the court, many of them first-offenders frequently engaged in simple stealing, the magistrates very seldom discharge a boy who has been found guilty. They use probation and fines in the usual way, although the former somewhat less and the latter somewhat more frequently, if compared with the mean, but they commit a considerable number of juveniles to Approved Schools. In Oxford County the picture of an unspectacular delinquency seems to be reflected in a treatment practice which resorts to discharge, probation, and fines in the usual way. Still within a normal range, however, the rate of fines is below the average as is the case in rural districts in general. In Newcastle, where every second boy before the court is a repeater, and where there is a good deal of delinquent activity among schoolboys resulting in other offences than simple stealing, and where there are indications of poverty in the families from which the delinquents come, there is a liberal use of absolute discharge and a normal use of conditional discharge, Approved Schools, and probation, though the latter remains below the district average and the industrial mean. In Swansea, where many young ordinary boys from stable families appear before the court for simple stealing, there is again a wide use of absolute discharge, a more or less normal use of conditional discharge, fines, and Approved Schools, but only a low rate of probation. In the West Riding, where magistrates are faced with numerous unfavourable reports on the boys' intelligence and character, where every second boy is charged with simple stealing, and where again one-half of the total of court cases are boys with previous court appearances, absolute discharge, Approved Schools, and fines occur at normal rates. Within this range, fines are more frequently used compared with the national and industrial means, while probation is applied at a very moderate rate only.

These observations lead to the final question whether there is any relationship between the delinquency situation which confronts the magistrates and the forms of treatment which they award. In theory, two principal solutions of this problem are feasible. Either there is a rational treatment policy where each decision is determined by a well-founded assessment of the individual's personal needs and prospects, with the result that the features of delinquency are reflected in a corresponding selection of suitable measures. Or else the magistrates follow certain traditional lines in preferring or disfavouring some of the measures at their disposal. In practice, one would expect that rational considerations coincide with traditional inclinations. It may also be that where certain forms of delinquency make it advisable for the magistrates to resort to specific measures, they show a preference for the same measures in other cases as well.

Relation between Delinquency and Treatment

If one surveys the evidence from all five districts as a whole, it becomes apparent that one rational consideration has been applied throughout. Adverse family conditions make it necessary to resort to a form of treatment by which the juvenile is separated from his home. Out of 490 boys from the five districts, for whom information on all relevant criminological data was available, 19 per cent. of the first-offenders and 25 per cent. of the repeaters came from families where at least one other member was concerned in criminal activities. This is generally regarded as a crime-promoting factor. More than this, it is a selective factor which determines the treatment practice of magistrates. The percentage of such boys among those put on probation was 19, but among those committed to Approved Schools, to the care of the local authority, or to punitive detention, it amounted to 35 per cent. When repeaters who come from homes with a criminal record appear before the court, magistrates have a strong motive for separating them from an unwholesome family atmosphere. While from a mere statistical analysis of relevant figures one would expect that 11 per cent. of the repeaters with crime in the family would be put on probation, actually only 5 per cent. were left to the probation officer's care. Conversely, while one would expect to find 22 per cent. of these boys to be removed from home, actually 26 per cent. were committed to Approved Schools, the local authority, or to punitive detention.

If one turns from general observations to the specific experience in individual localities, one finds in the figures for Oxford a confirmation of these considerations. In Oxford, where 27 out of 100 boys before the court are older boys from broken homes, the magistrates make many committals to Approved Schools. In Oxford County a non-spectacular delinquency is treated in a way which corresponds to the practice which is normally applied elsewhere. The magistrates in Newcastle, Swansea, and the West Riding are confronted with a more formidable amount of delinquency, although only the West Riding has been classified as a high-delinquency area. In these three districts, the obvious problem for the Bench seems to be the question of how to distinguish between those offenders who do, and those who do not, need a measure involving a personal treatment. In Newcastle, where many schoolboys, even repeaters, frequently from poor homes, appear before the court, the magistrates use few fines but are also reluctant to order probation. In Swansea, with numerous ordinary schoolboys from stable homes concerned in simple stealing, the magistrates use probation only sparingly. In the West Riding, a high-delinquency area with many older repeaters, magistrates make a fair use of fines and again only a small use of probation. These are some indications of the ways in which these three districts react to a fairly high delinquency with certain different measures. Beyond these subtle differences all three districts dispose of a considerable number of their court cases by absolute discharge.

Within the range of this limited experience, the evidence shows certain common lines of present-day treatment policy, but also certain local differences in the sense that similar measures are sometimes applied to different cases, or different measures to similar cases. On the basis of a very extensive material, such evidence could well be used as an experiment *ex post*. It would be misleading to compare reconviction-rates of courts with different treatment practice unless the differences in the amount and forms of delinquency were taken into account. A comparison, however, of reconviction-rates of similar criminological types who had been awarded different forms of penal and corrective treatment would be a fair test. The difficulties of such an undertaking are obvious. For any reliable conclusions, a statistical evaluation of very large numbers of case studies is required. If, however, these numerous cases are collected over a number of years, the conditions of the experiment no longer remain the same. Typical features of delinquency as well as the efficiency of institutional and non-institutional treatment never remain stable, but are in a constant process of development and change. Within the framework of the present investigation, only certain illustrations can be given in order to support a number of working hypotheses. A record of reconvictions or otherwise was used as a test of failure or success, cases were followed up from the period between the court appearance between 1948 and 1950 which was relevant for their inclusion into this survey, and the time when the fieldwork was done in the winter of 1952–3. One further reservation must be made. Where Approved School cases are included in groups used for the comparison of reconviction-rates, one has to remember that during their stay in Approved Schools juveniles do not share the criminal risks of their contemporaries in the world at large. These facts give the statements which follow a merely tentative character. Beyond the immediate purpose of illustrating certain points of the present discussion, these observations are intended to suggest the lines on which future research in this direction should be undertaken.

Testing the Result of Different Ways of Treatment

The first general impression of the after-conduct of delinquents who had undergone the treatment awarded to them by the juvenile court is that its success and failure go hand in hand with the less or more serious character of the offence. The serious or less serious character of a theft committed by a juvenile depends on four factors: the way in which it is committed, the place from which the objects are stolen, the type of object, and its value. The most serious cases are those where a boy has stolen (*a*) by breaking and entering, (*b*) from enclosed premises, (*c*) money, clothes, jewellery, or watches, (*d*) to the value of £5 or over. At the other end of the scale would be a case of (*a*) simple stealing, (*b*) from vehicles, outside a building, or otherwise not from enclosed premises, (*c*) of sweets, playthings, food, cycles, (*d*) to the value of less than £5. For the sake of statistical analysis, a case with at least two elements of a serious theft was assessed as a harmful offence and a case with no more than one serious element as a less harmful offence. Out of 337 cases of theft by boys where sufficient relevant information was available, 146 were harmful and 191 less harmful offences. The reconviction rate of boys guilty of these less harmful offences was 37 per cent. and of boys who had committed the more harmful offences 43 per cent. The difference in the actual after-effects of treatment between boys guilty of harmful and less harmful offences is even more notable than the figures suggest. Since 11·6 of the first and only 8·3 of the second type of offenders were removed from their homes by committal to Approved Schools or local authorities or by detention in a Remand Home, a greater number of boys guilty of less harmful offences were exposed to the risks of life at large for a longer time.

While the impact of the boy's criminality on the prospects of readjustment is far from being insignificant, his personal circumstances and home background are even more important for the selection of treatment and its possible effects. For an appropriate assessment, it was assumed that five factors characterize a bad personal background. They are (*a*) a broken home, (*b*) disharmony in the family, (*c*) lack of discipline in the family, (*d*) crime in the family, (*e*) a personal history of maladjustment. This is the same configuration which has been used in one of the preceding sections in order to characterize typical forms of delinquency in the five selected districts. For the present purpose of calculating correlations between the offender's personal background and the success and failure of his treatment, the five factors were grouped in a different way. In this context a boy would have a good personal background if he came (*a*) from a complete natural family, with (*b*) no disharmony, (*c*) no lack of discipline, (*d*) no crime in the family, and (*e*) with no record of his own previous maladjustment, but it would be assumed that he had an unsatisfactory personal background if he was affected by at least one of those five adverse factors. Among 566 boys about whom relevant information was available, 249 had a good and 317 an unsatisfactory personal background. In the end, 30 per cent. of the good and 43 per cent. of the unsatisfactory boys were reconvicted. The striking identity of the reconviction-rates of boys guilty of harmful offences and with an unsatisfactory personal background is more apparent than real. Actually the prospects of readjustment for boys with an unsatisfactory personal background are even less favourable than the reconviction-rate of 43 per cent. indicates. Only 3·2 per cent. of the boys with a good personal background, but 21·9 per cent. of those with an unsatisfactory personal background, were committed to Approved Schools, local authorities, or to detention in a Remand Home. The reconviction-rate of 43 refers, therefore, to a group of boys, of whom a considerable proportion was for only a short time exposed to the risk of crime in a life at large.

With this reservation, the figures illustrate two further points. The first observation refers to the treatment practice of the magistrates. The figures show that where committals are made to Approved Schools, local authorities, or to detention in Remand Homes, magistrates are influenced by the boys' personal background rather than by the serious nature of the offence. Among boys found guilty of harmful offences, whatever their personal background, 11·6 per cent. were removed from their homes, but among those with an unsatisfactory personal background, whatever their offence, the percentage was 21·9. A treatment which involves the separation of a boy from his home is therefore used not as a punitive measure for a particular offence, but as a necessary step towards overcoming the causes of maladjustment which have their roots in his personal background. In numerous cases the unwholesome influence of bad family conditions is the principal reason for the magistrates' decision to remove a juvenile offender from his home. These considerations are confirmed by practical results. Educative treatment away from an unfavourable home has proved reasonably successful. On the limited evidence available, among boys committed to the local authority, to an Approved School, or to detention in a Remand Home, success and failure are almost evenly spread among boys from families where at least one other member was concerned in crime, and from families without such difficulties. There were 7 reconvictions among 28 boys with crime in the family, and 12 reconvictions among 50 boys with no crime in the family.

The second comment on the results of present treatment practice is that the nature of the offence is less significant for the outcome than the quality of the boy's personal background. The success-rate of boys with a good personal background, whatever their offence, is higher than the success-rate of boys guilty of only a less harmful offence, whatever their personal background. At the same time, the prospect of failure for boys with a bad personal background is greater than for boys guilty of more harmful offences. While the statistical analysis results in a reconviction-rate of 43 per cent. for both groups, the higher proportion of committals to Approved Schools among boys with a bad personal background reduces the time at risk for a greater number of this group, and for this reason their actual prospects of failure are higher than is indicated by the reconviction-rates which cover the time when they were staying in an institution.

The evidence collected from the five selected districts throws some light also on the vexed question of absolute and conditional discharge with which the preceding discussion was confronted at various times. The first impression is that discharge within the normal limits of its application does not fare too badly if compared with the after-effects of other forms of treatment. Among 102 delinquent boys who had been absolutely discharged, 62 did not commit further offences during the time under observation, and among 189 put on probation, 114 had no further offences. The success depends, as always, on the selection of the right type of offender for a specific treatment. If the investigation is concentrated on a particular type of delinquent, success and failure are less evenly distributed between different forms of treatment. On the strength of the present evidence, boys with a previous court appearance have a 53 per cent. prospect of success in terms of absence of further offences in the comparatively short follow-up period. Out of 70 probationers with previous convictions, 35 did not appear before the court again. Likewise, in the 20 cases which appeared to the court trifling enough to be disposed of by absolute discharge in spite of the boys' previous offences, 11 did not appear before the court again within the prescribed period. Among other 20 repeaters, however, who had been conditionally discharged, only 6 were free from further offences.

The last figures suggest the need for constructive treatment methods where the courts have to deal with delinquents who show symptoms of a more lasting maladjustment as it is indicated, among other factors, by repeated criminal activities. This point comes out more clearly if one examines the way in which different courts use absolute and conditional discharge for repeaters. Relevant figures in Table XXXII lead to two conclusions. First, they show that the high rates of discharge in Newcastle and Swansea are not the result of inflated numbers of trifling cases which swell the court register, but are rather the outcome of a deliberate treatment policy. In both places, the large number of delinquents who were discharged included a high proportion of repeaters. Secondly, the reconviction-rate was higher in these two places where a liberal use of discharge extended this measure to a fairly large number of repeaters. In Oxford County and the West Riding, however, where magistrates made no more than a fair or moderate use of discharge and included only a small proportion of repeaters, reconviction-rates of boys who had previously been discharged were notably smaller.

TABLE XXXII. *Percentage Rates of Discharge with reference to Repeaters and Further Offences among Delinquent Boys in Five Selected Districts*

District	(*a*) *Absolute discharge*	(*b*) *Conditional discharge*	*Total of* $a+b$	*Rate of boys with previous offences and discharged*	*Rate of boys discharged and committing further offences*
Oxford . .	—	1	1	—	1
Oxford County	14	13	27	5	3
Newcastle .	37	6	43	15	25
Swansea .	35	19	54	15	28
W. Riding .	19	9	28	6	6
National mean	21·0	10·0	31·0	—	—

These observations point to the way in which ultimately the results of these experiments *ex post* are to be evaluated, and suggest how the relative success of different treatment practices can be assessed. The decisive test is the after-conduct of juvenile delinquents of a comparable criminological type under different treatment practices. For reasons discussed on several occasions above, the present material allows no more than certain tentative suggestions. Since very little has been done on these lines so far, it might be justified to offer some conclusions which can be drawn from the evidence hitherto available. In the discussion on results of the treatment awarded in the courts of all five selected districts together, the investigation was concentrated on four types of delinquent boys: boys guilty of harmful offences, and boys guilty of less harmful offences, whatever their personal background, and boys with a good or unsatisfactory personal background, whatever their offences. Tables XXXIII and XXXIV show local success rates in terms of absence of further convictions for these four types of delinquent boys in each of the five districts which have different treatment practices as described in preceding sections of this chapter.

TABLE XXXIII. *Success and Failure related to Types of Offence in Five Selected Districts*

	Oxford		Oxford County		Newcastle		Swansea		W. Riding	
	No.	%	No.	%	No.	%	No.	%	No.	%
4, 3, or 2 bad factors										
Success . .	11	64	6	60	13	40	18	58	36	64
Failure . .	6	36	4	40	19	60	13	42	20	36
1 bad factor										
Success . .	18	70	27	93	13	50	17	39	46	70
Failure . .	8	30	2	7	13	50	27	61	20	30

Number of boys in this enumeration 337.

TABLE XXXIV. *Success and Failure related to Home Background of 566 Boys before the Courts of Five Selected Districts*

	Oxford		Oxford County		Newcastle		Swansea		W. Riding	
Any single factor bad	No.	%	No.	%	No.	%	No.	%	No.	%
Success . .	34	62	25	75	23	47	18	35	81	62
Failure . .	21	38	8	25	26	53	33	65	48	38
All factors good										
Success . .	24	80	44	95	22	53	29	66	59	67
Failure . .	6	20	2	5	19	47	15	34	29	33

An interpretation of these figures leads to the following considerations. With regard to boys guilty of harmful offences, there seems to be no apparent connexion between a particular treatment practice and the local success-rate. The success-rate of boys guilty of harmful offences ranges between 64 per cent. in Oxford and the West Riding and 40 per cent. in Newcastle. In Oxford the high success-rate could be explained by the sparing use of discharge and the frequent committals to Approved Schools which, apart from any beneficial after-effects, keep the boys out of risk. In the West Riding, however, magistrates are generous with absolute discharge, use Approved Schools not more than to an average extent, and put comparatively few delinquents on probation. While these two different patterns of treatment practice coincide with the same high standard of success in spite of considerable criminality, Newcastle seems to be less successful with a similar though even more abundant use of absolute discharge, with a use of probation somewhat between the incidence in Oxford and the West Riding, and a sparing application of fines. At the other end of the scale, boys guilty of less harmful offences seem to succeed almost without exception in Oxford County, but at a rate of only 39 per cent. in Swansea. Here the fact that Swansea uses more absolute discharge and less probation may offer a clue. In respect of the third type, boys with an unsatisfactory personal background, success ranges between 75 per cent. in Oxford County and no more than 35 per cent. in Swansea. This leads to the question whether the abundance of absolute discharge and the sparing use of probation affects the prospects of readjustment for difficult boys and for minor offenders alike. In the final and most hopeful group, delinquent boys with a good personal background, there is a range of success between nearly all the cases in Oxford County and 53 per cent. in Newcastle. While the treatment practice in Oxfordshire is a more or less true reflection of what is typical in England and Wales in general, Newcastle makes abundant use of absolute discharge.

These associations between success and failure in the social adjustment of comparable types of offenders on the one hand and certain patterns of treatment practice on the other, point to the relative merits or otherwise of one or the other form of penal and corrective measures. The reduction of the case material to more or less homogeneous offender groups alone does not permit the isolation of the treatment factor as a probable cause of the delinquent's good or bad after-conduct. If, in rural Oxfordshire, delinquency-rates in general are lower than in industrial places like Newcastle and Swansea, one would expect less crime also among those who had already been before the court, and this might occur independently of the treatment awarded to them. The 'experiments *ex post*' do not take place under completely controlled conditions. No two districts are entirely equal in all relevant aspects.

With these reservations, three conclusions can be drawn from the experience gained in the five districts under review. The first impression is a confirmation of the view sometimes expressed by competent observers, that, on the whole, the courts make the right use of measures which imply a removal of the young delinquent from his home. To separate a child or a young person from his home is not only an infringement of the personal rights and liberties both of the child and his parents, but also something which, at least at the outset, means a considerable hardship for the boy or girl who has never been away from home. As a rule, magistrates do not use these measures for their implied punitive effect. The decisive factor is the quality of the family home, not the gravity of the offence. The results seem to justify this policy.

When there is no need for removing a young law-breaker from his home, a second question arises. Magistrates have to decide how far constructive personal treatment is necessary, or whether it would be sufficient to dispose of the case by taking no action at all, or by employing a sanction with no personal appeal to the juvenile. It is the question of probation on the one hand and of discharge and fines on the other. Since 1950 committal to an Attendance Centre is available as a further form of personal treatment. Experience with these measures differs greatly, especially with regard to less serious offences, which are sometimes committed by juveniles with a good personal background. It is indeed difficult to know where, in such circumstances, an ill-advised action would only interfere with an otherwise healthy process of adjustment and the gaining of maturity, and where, on the contrary, there is, behind the deceptive surface of a trifling offence, an urgent need for preventive action. The evidence strengthens the view, at least as a working hypothesis, that in places where a considerable proportion of delinquents is disposed of by absolute or conditional discharge there is, among these young offenders, a number who would fare much better under the constructive methods of probation. This applies primarily to boys with personal difficulties and family problems, but this group extends far into the realm of more or less harmless petty delinquency. Here is an immediate task for further criminological studies, to find out more about the needs and prospects of problem children with unproblematical delinquency. So far, we know very little about the psychological effect of fines, either upon a boy or upon his parents. The evidence suggests the possibility that fines might be used to advantage in the case of delinquents with a good personal background.

The third comment is that there is no conclusive evidence to show what would be the best treatment policy with regard to the serious forms of juvenile crime. The reason why a comparison of local experience alone does not throw sufficient light on this problem, lies probably in the complex nature of what we call serious criminality. Even if this concept is not used in a formal legal sense, but, as in the present context, applies to results of a criminological classification of the underlying facts, delinquency of a comparable type and gravity can be the outcome of quite different psychological situations. For this reason different ways of treatment may be called for. It would be interesting to resume comparisons of local practice and corresponding results when more experience with the new measures in the armoury of the courts is available. The new measure of detention in a detention centre introduced by section 18 of the Criminal Justice Act, 1948, is intended to fill the gap where no long-term educative efforts, either institutional or extra-mural, are advisable, but an impressive action is necessary in order to prevent a further development into persistent and dangerous forms of criminality.

CHAPTER V

FURTHER OUTLOOK

Lessons of the Post-war Experience

JUVENILE delinquency and the treatment of young offenders are not the concern of lawyers and social workers alone. They are important features of the life of the community, and indeed the work of the juvenile courts receives much attention from the general public. In questions of human behaviour and the reactions of the community to it, everybody claims to have his own opinion. Obviously, it is often a subjective judgement which determines the statements of individual observers on favourable or appalling conditions of the young generation and on desirable or deplorable tendencies in the practice of the courts. The student of delinquent youth welcomes any expression of personal interest in these matters where it springs from a sense of social responsibility. Even where such general opinions are not based on a full knowledge of relevant facts, they sometimes point in the right direction. It is the purpose of empirical criminological studies to separate truth from prejudice and to present the facts which allow for unbiased statements about the delinquency situation and the actual or possible effects of penal and corrective treatment. Juvenile delinquency is a field in which much discussion is going on but where few sensational new discoveries can be expected. Where the motivations of human actions and reactions are the issue, there will never be a complete and unchallengable answer. Behaviour sciences are still in their initial stage. Criminological studies are intended to discard ill-founded propositions, to verify certain assumptions, and to make it clear within what limits our knowledge of the extent and nature of criminal conduct and the effect of certain treatment methods and other factors is borne out by empirical evidence. Only by such modest but painstaking efforts, where subsequent studies are built upon the results of preceding research, can we hope to advance to a deeper understanding of the perennial problems of crime and punishment.[1]

As a contribution to the social history of post-war Britain the present study presents certain lessons from the experience of juvenile delinquency and the treatment practice of the courts in a typical post-war triennium. The evidence produced confirms the general impression of a probable increase and, at any rate, a considerable extent of juvenile delinquency during that period. The search for causes of juvenile delinquency in general and of the high tide of post-war delinquency with the three-year rhythm in particular has lost something of its topical interest. Criminology has not been able to go beyond Sir Cyril Burt's principle of 'multiple causation'. It is the proposition that the criminal activities of an individual no less than delinquency as a social mass phenomenon are never due to a single principal cause, but must be explained by a coincidence of diverse personal and social factors, each of which can occur among non-delinquents as well. Criminological interest today has shifted from the causes of crime to the effects of treatment. However, even such treatment research must not lose sight of the characteristics of the juvenile delinquents who appear before the courts and are put on probation or committed to institutions, and of any changes in the types of young offender with whom magistrates and social workers have to deal. The present survey has shown that the problems confronting the magistrates differ qualitatively in different localities. In a similar way the magistrates' tasks change in the course of time. A local study of the delinquency of girls in Oxford, covering the years 1933–46, suggested that there have been three different periods of delinquency, each with its characteristic forms.[2] The pre-war period had a prevalence of what are called typical court cases, a hard core of seriously maladjusted girls with difficult character traits, bad work records, of whom many came from families where other members, too, had a criminal record. In the first years of the war the high tide of delinquency threw up a greater

[1] R. M. Jackson, *The Machinery of Justice in England* (2nd edn., 1953), pp. 173, 192, 202.

[2] Mary C. Grain, 'Recent Trends in the Delinquency of Girls', unpublished Oxford thesis, 1949. For experience of the first war years in London, see Eileen Younghusband, 6 *Howard Journal* (1941), 18.

proportion of girls with good character traits who swelled the ranks of incidental offenders; but among the seriously maladjusted girls too there was a remarkable number with a better educational standard and a satisfactory family background. In the later war years and the immediate post-war period there was less incidental delinquency by more or less well adjusted girls, but a deterioration in school records and work habits among the growing numbers of seriously maladjusted girls. Apparently social and economic conditions during this third period offered serious temptations to girls who by their character and way of life were ill-protected against the alluring glamour of illicit activities. At the same time, there was before the Oxford Juvenile Court a significant number of innocent victims of neglect and cruelty in conformity with the general increase in convictions for neglect and cruelty which, for the country as a whole, rose from 751 in 1939 to 1,634 in 1945 (non-indictable offences).

Ever since the lawlessness of youth has been discussed, it has often been said that delinquency is most spectacular in big industrial places. The present study confirms this view, not in the sense that every big city is invariably a high-delinquency area and none of the rural counties shows more than negligible crime-rates, but rather as a general pattern which can be regarded as typical. From whatever angle the facts are viewed, the same industrial places and maritime ports, mostly in the north-west and north-east of the country, came into the picture, characterized by high delinquency-rates and the prevalence of other unfavourable social factors. This result seems difficult to reconcile with the often-heard criticism that the present social services are too much modelled on the needs and possibilities of the big cities and too little adapted to the conditions in wide and thinly populated rural areas. In America, where the development of ecological studies facilitates efforts to concentrate the operation of social services on the danger spots, the unbroken continuity of high delinquency-rates in certain localities has been interpreted as further evidence of the supreme importance of the family factor in explaining the social maladjustment of youth. Those families who are unable to emancipate themselves from a slum environment are the same as those who are not capable of bringing up their children unharmed by the adverse conditions around them.[1] While these observations should not be unduly generalized, they certainly show the direction in which social services must work if they are to reduce youthful lawlessness and other undesirable social conditions in high-delinquency areas. They confirm once again the present shift of emphasis, in social studies and in social work, from external circumstances to the human factor.

In times when the numbers of young offenders increase and juvenile delinquency becomes a topical subject of general discussion there is much opportunity for studying the treatment methods available and their effect on young law-breakers. The experience of the post-war years as it has been surveyed in the present study points in two directions. On the one hand, it shows how important it is to recognize the early beginnings of serious maladjustment even beneath the harmless surface of trifling offences. This is the case of the problem child with non-problematical delinquency. In large areas with a considerable number of delinquents magistrates often have no choice but to dispose of a good deal of what appear to be less serious cases by granting a discharge or imposing a fine in order to be able to concentrate on more serious cases. In the circumstances such selective practice is certainly appropriate, but then our methods of diagnosis and classification need further development and refinement. New research in this direction might gain much from a comparative study of methods used and experience acquired in observation centres abroad, for which the First International Course on Criminology in Paris, 1952, was a good beginning.[2] For a differential diagnosis of minor first offenders it would be essential to know who are—according to pre-war experience—the 70 per cent. of boys of 16 and 17 years of age and the 86 per cent. of girls who after their first convictions do not appear before the court again, and who are the 30 and 14 per cent. respectively who join the ranks of recidivists.[3] Any progress in the direction of such differentiation would make it easier to apply constructive methods in cases where a deliberate

[1] Paul Tappan, *Comparative Survey of Juvenile Delinquency. Part I. North America* (United Nations, 1952), p. 101.

[2] G. Heuyer and J. Pinatel, *L'Examen médico-psychologique et social des Délinquants*, Paris, 1953.

[3] *Criminal Statistics, England and Wales 1938*, pp. xxi and xxvi.

remedial effort is necessary in order to prevent the young law-breaker from further wrongdoing.

Like most other critical studies of treatment methods and their effects on juvenile offenders the present survey confirms the impression that we are still far from a solution of the baffling problem of how to overcome serious and deep-rooted forms of persistent delinquency. Two specific issues have recently raised increasing attention. On the one hand, there has been a deeper understanding of the social approach to crime and delinquency. The emphasis is no longer on the 'reformation' of the individual still seen in isolation like a prisoner in his cell, but on 'adjustment', a sociological concept which includes man's relationship to his environment and points to the need for a two-way process of mutual adaptation between the individual and his personal surroundings. We have learnt that slum clearance is more than a mere problem of architecture and that it requires due regard paid to spiritual needs and the demands for a full natural life within a sound organic community. The exemplary work of the Family Service Units has shown the way to a comprehensive teamwork approach to persistent forms of maladjustment which are due to family problems rather than to faults and failures of individuals who could be singled out to bear alone the responsibility for their shortcomings. On the other hand, the growing extension of medical psychology far beyond the sphere of mental disease and insanity has led to a deeper insight into the close affinity between psychopathic personalities and persistent wrongdoing, although in this field, as in many others, diagnosis appears to be far ahead of therapy. However, even if full consideration is given to preventive efforts in these two directions, there still remains a broad middle ground where in one way or another the magistrates must take action in the face of persistent delinquency. The question arises whether any lesson can be learnt from the experience gained at different places with different modes of treatment.

In order to answer this question, a further differentiation is necessary. The concept of persistent delinquency refers to a repetition of lawless activities and to consistent anti-social behaviour. It implies also the commission of offences of a certain serious kind by a juvenile whose personal characteristics reveal symptoms of a lasting social maladjustment. The gravity of the offence committed, which was the dominating factor under a retributive system, seems to have lost a good deal of its significance in recent criminological discussions. The evidence of the present survey suggests that, in cases of theft, success and failure in the delinquent's readjustment are, to a certain extent, related to the gravity of the offence. This observation applies independently of the particular treatment practice of different courts. However, the discussion of the previous chapter has shown that the delinquent's personal circumstances and home background are even more significant than the gravity of the offence. Magistrates resort to a committal to an Approved School not for the punitive effect of an enforced separation from the family, but in order to prevent further deterioration caused by the influence of a bad home. Such a practice keeps a number of boys with a high crime-risk out of trouble for a while. The effects of long-term institutional treatment can only be assessed after a long follow-up period. The Approved School could in fairness claim a successful result for its treatment even if in the end it was only the natural forces of a belated process of gaining maturity that brought stability and a healthy purpose into the life of young law-breakers. Where delinquency is closely associated with unfavourable personal circumstances, there is an urgent need for constructive measures. Such a statement may be a truism, but the evidence produced confirms, by practical experience, that a district making a frequent use of discharge and a sparing use of probation has a smaller success rate for boys with a bad personal background than other areas under observation. This result points to the desirability of a more frequent use of probation and a full development of its possibilities in connexion with conditions of residence in homes and hostels and with child guidance and other forms of medical treatment. Further experience is needed to show how far an Attendance Centre offers an opportunity for combining a punitive purpose with constructive treatment.

Throughout the entire investigation, the discussion has centred upon the juvenile court. In the Children Act, 1908, and the Children and Young Persons Act, 1933, the juvenile court was designed as the institution to deal primarily and exclusively with wayward and delinquent youth. The education of the public to recognize and accept this comprehensive function has succeeded to such an extent that the rising number of recorded juvenile delinquents is partly due to the fact that children are brought before the courts whose behaviour was previously reprimanded at home, at school, or by the policeman on the beat, or just dismissed with a shrug of the shoulder and a sigh of indignation. The flexibility of procedure and of the measures applicable, which the juvenile court has in common with other social and legal institutions in England, has further facilitated this process. For forty years the juvenile court was alone in the field beside the local education authority, until in 1948 the Children's Officer was established as a counterpart in the related sphere of child care. This historical development explains the fact that before English juvenile courts criminal responsibility begins at the unusually early age of 8 years, and this fact again contributes to the non-punitive atmosphere which is more prevalent in English juvenile courts than in some of the continental countries where children of compulsory school age are not subject to a criminal jurisdiction. As to the future of juvenile courts in England, the results of this study offer some evidence for two considerations. The first concerns the question whether the court should maintain its exclusive jurisdiction over every case of juvenile misbehaviour, or whether a sifting machinery should be established to keep certain cases out of court and to provide alternative methods of handling juvenile waywardness and petty delinquency.[1] A reform on such lines would assign to the courts those cases where a judicial decision is expected and required, but would spare from appearance in court many of those against whom at present the court itself thinks it best to take no action at all. More than every third child and every fourth young person found guilty of an indictable offence are discharged by the magistrates. This survey has thrown some light on the criminological significance of these figures, in respect of local variations and qualitative differences among juvenile delinquents absolutely or conditionally discharged. In Carmarthen, Newcastle upon Tyne, and Swansea, more than every second juvenile offender found guilty of an indictable offence is discharged, either absolutely or conditionally, while in Huddersfield and Halifax less than one in twenty-

[1] H. Mannheim in M. Fry and others, *Lawless Youth* (1947), pp. 52–56.

five cases escapes with a mere discharge. High discharge figures cover a number of cases 'informally adjusted' by appropriate arrangements voluntarily accepted by the parents, other cases where as a matter of treatment policy the magistrates deliberately refrain from any positive action, but undoubtedly also many trifling cases not suitable to be dealt with before a court of law. A high proportion of court cases ending with a discharge weakens the healthy fear inspired by the juvenile court and accustoms the young law-breaker gradually to the not too unpleasant experience of a court appearance. These observations support the traditional practice of police cautioning, but the evidence produced in Chapter III shows that this practice is far from being uniform throughout the whole country, nor is it consistent over longer periods in places where it is used. The question of a sifting machinery therefore requires a fresh examination in principle.

The second consideration points in the opposite direction. If, as a result of future reforms, the juvenile court loses a certain proportion of minor cases of juveniles of tender years, it may gain in an extended jurisdiction over higher age groups. Recent legislation in the United States and in Germany made provision for specific forms of procedure and treatment in respect of adolescent offenders. The present survey has only touched this problem, but even the few relevant observations gave the impression that the criminality of adolescents, that is minors over juvenile court age, differs from juvenile delinquency and adult criminality both in its trend in the course of time and in its local distribution. This experience confirms the impression that adolescent criminality has its own typical problems and makes it doubtful whether the seventeenth birthday should indeed constitute such a rigid dividing line between the state of a juvenile and the full application of adult criminal law.

The Subsiding Tide of Delinquency

In the social sciences every study has the character of an interim report. Any extension of knowledge and any progress in understanding tend to raise new questions which require further research and fresh solutions. At the same time, the subject-matter of social studies is constantly changing. Life in the community with its continuous interplay of personal relationships never comes to a standstill. This general observation applies also to the selected topics of juvenile delinquency and the treatment practice of the courts. As the years go by the post-war period is seen in its proper perspective. The subordinate relation of time and events to the war which is implied in the expression 'post-war' has come to an end. We now see fluctuations and trends of social phenomena in the light of more recent conditions. Social problems today have at last become topics in their own right.

Ten years after the end of the war, the general impression prevails that the high tide of juvenile delinquency in England and Wales is subsiding. For the large number of delinquent boys, the last of the three post-war peaks, the year 1951, remained an unprecedented and unrepeated record of criminal activities. The national crime-rate per 100,000 junior boys fell from the high-water mark of 1,503 in 1951 to 1,336 in 1952, and reached, with the figure of 1,122 in 1953, a level below any corresponding figure since 1940. Likewise the crime-rate for senior boys dropped from the spectacular record figure of 2,044 in 1951 to 1,981 in 1952 and to 1,663 in 1953, a rate below the figures of early war delinquency in 1940 and 1941. The small numbers of delinquent girls show a less characteristic picture. For the junior girls the second of the three post-war peaks, the year 1948, had the record crime-rate of 123; the rate of 119 in 1951 dropped only slowly to 117 in 1952 and then fell to 98 in 1953, a figure still above all yearly rates before 1948 with the exception of the unusually high figure of 100 for 1943. The senior girls had their record year in 1941 with a crime-rate of 216, reached their moderate third post-war peak of 210 only in 1952, and fell back slowly to 192 in 1953.

For an interpretation of these figures the recent trends in crime and delinquency must be followed up in the local sphere. According to the Report of the Metropolitan Police, crime in the Metropolis reached its highest level in the post-war years 1944–8. The moderate peak in 1951 was followed by a steady decrease in the rate of indictable offences recorded by the police per 1,000 inhabitants of Greater London which in 1953 with a figure of 11·9 and in 1954 with a figure of 11·27 was only slightly above the pre-war standard of 10–11. Within this general falling trend the numbers of juveniles arrested by the police decreased between 1952 and 1953 by 8·1 per cent. for children and 11·3 for young persons, although the arrests of juveniles in 1953 still exceeded the pre-war standard of 1938 by 32·7 per cent. for children and 15·5 per cent. for young persons.[1]

Table XXXV illustrates the recent tendencies of delinquency in the local sphere by annual numbers of juvenile delinquents in certain selected areas. According to these figures, high-delinquency areas furnish no exception to the apparent decrease in the number of young offenders. The number of delinquent girls for a single year in a single locality is too small to indicate any characteristic trend. With regard to the boys, there is in Bootle, Liverpool, and Middlesbrough the gradual decrease which one would expect on the strength of the national delinquency-rates. Birkenhead reached the reduction of 1953 only after a further increase in 1952. Grimsby, however, presents a different picture. There the fall after the local peak of 1952 was only moderate and leaves the number of delinquent junior boys and of girls still above the 1951 level. A comparison between two high-probation areas and two areas with a frequent use of fines shows no spectacular difference in the way they followed the national trend. The small numbers of cases for single years do not allow of any far-reaching conclusions from the fluctuations between one year and another. Whatever the reasons for the recent flattening-out of the delinquency curve, they seem to be independent of the preference of local magistrates for one or the other treatment practice.

In Scotland the curve of juvenile delinquency during the post-war years shows a similar picture of a three-year rhythm, though the variations are less marked than in England. The high-water mark of juvenile delinquency in Scotland coincided with the end of the war, 1945, when the number of crimes proved against juveniles exceeded the pre-war figure for 1938 by 50 per cent. There were moderate peaks in 1948 and in the biennium 1951–2 with increases above the pre-war level between 26·7 and 28·9 per cent. The delinquency-rates in Table XXXVI are the nearest possible figures for a comparison with rates of persons found guilty of indictable offences in England.

[1] *Report of the Commissioner of Police of the Metropolis for the Year 1953*; *The Times*, 21 Jan. 1955.

TABLE XXXV. *Number of Juveniles found Guilty of Indictable Offences in Selected Areas, 1951–3*

District	Boys 8–13	Boys 14–17	Girls 8–13	Girls 14–17	All Juveniles 8–17
			High-delinquency areas		
Bootle					
1951 . .	132	59	8	3	202
1952 . .	83	51	12	7	153
1953 . .	82	41	10	2	135
Birkenhead					
1951 . .	200	97	19	9	325
1952 . .	243	107	14	15	379
1953 . .	153	79	12	9	253
Liverpool					
1951 . .	1,314	679	64	94	2,151
1952 . .	916	631	70	98	1,715
1953 . .	773	507	46	66	1,392
Grimsby					
1951 . .	125	46	9	2	182
1952 . .	143	43	14	8	208
1953 . .	141	33	13	11	198
Middlesbrough					
1951 . .	241	110	24	24	399
1952 . .	189	74	30	13	306
1953 . .	194	74	21	19	308
			High-probation areas		
Halifax					
1951 . .	50	44	3	—	97
1952 . .	44	20	5	4	73
1953 . .	50	46	8	3	107
Huddersfield					
1951 . .	50	30	9	8	97
1952 . .	79	48	4	6	137
1953 . .	46	37	4	2	89
			High-fine areas		
Rotherham					
1951 . .	63	37	11	11	122
1952 . .	63	51	8	3	125
1953 . .	48	43	8	4	103
Blackburn					
1951 . .	43	44	1	1	89
1952 . .	61	41	1	1	104
1953 . .	43	25	2	—	70

The figures for Scotland are based on the number of boys and girls against whom a charge of crime was proved, in the meaning which this term has in Scots law, but with the exclusion of crimes of class IV, that is malicious injuries to property, most

TABLE XXXVI. *Delinquency-rates in Scotland. Crimes proved, excluding Class IV, per 1,000 Boys and Girls aged 8–17*

	Boys	*Girls*
1949 . .	17·8	1·4
1950 . .	20·0	1·4
1951 . .	21·5	1·9
1952 . .	22·3	1·8
1953 . .	18·8	1·8

of which are non-indictable offences in English law.[1] The figures suggest a certain consistency in the delinquency situation in Scotland, but there appears to be a notable fall in the crime-rates of boys from 1952 to 1953, though they still remain above the figures for 1949.

TABLE XXXVII. *France. Number of Juveniles 13–18 found Guilty, 1949–52*

	Paris	*Provincial France*
1949 . .	5,253	15,932
1950 . .	4,762	13,182
1951 . .	2,866	12,105
1952 . .	2,561	12,063

As an illustration of recent conditions abroad, the observations which follow refer to three continental countries. In France[2] there was, as the figures in Table XXXVII suggest, a dramatic fall by more than one-half the total of juvenile offenders in the capital between 1949 and 1952. This notable decrease in the numbers of delinquents is partly due to a reduction in the comparatively high incidence of delinquency among girls. In 1951 there

[1] Figures computed from *Criminal Statistics, Scotland.* For the preceding years see also A. M. Struthers, *Measuring Bad Behaviour*, published by the National Council of Social Service, 1950.

[2] Ministère de la Justice, *Direction de la éducation surveillée, Rapport Annuel*, 1952, p. 11, and 1953, p. 10.

were in France two delinquent girls for every nine delinquent boys. The general moderate decrease from 1951 to 1952 was entirely due to a fall in the number of delinquent girls which more than compensated for a slight increase in the number of delinquent boys. While the number of boys increased from 12,213 in 1951 to 12,415 in 1952, the corresponding numbers for girls decreased from 2,785 to 2,209.

TABLE XXXVIII. *Switzerland. Number of Juveniles of no more than 17 found Guilty*

	Boys	*Girls*
1945	863	142
1946	714	120
1947	725	101
1948	779	135
1949	753	122
1950	699	115
1951	682	111
1952	795	107
1953	664	135

In Switzerland,[1] according to the figures reproduced in Table XXXVIII, juvenile delinquency has decreased or at least has reached a stable condition on a level below the peak which coincided with the year of the end of the war, 1945. This is the result of a specific trend in juvenile delinquency, since for all other age groups the number of convictions in 1953 was higher than in 1945. The crime-rate for adults of 18 and over per 100,000 rose from 864·8 in 1945 to 930·3 in 1953. Like the English figures, the yearly numbers of convicted boys in Switzerland show three post-war peaks, though not with a three-year rhythm; the Swiss peak years were 1945, 1948, and 1952. These are the same years in which some of the districts in England and Wales had their highest crime figures, as indicated in Table XXXV. This experience lends some support to the opinion of observers who explain the mysterious three-year rhythm in the national figures for England and Wales not by a new unknown recurrent cause of delinquency, but by a mere chance variation.

The crime situation in the German Federal Republic took

[1] *Statistisches Jahrbuch der Schweiz*, 1953, p. 525.

a dramatic turn almost to the day, when in 1948 the currency reform ended the immediate post-war state of utter economic distress and complete social disintegration, and reinstated money as the most coveted commodity. In North Rhine-Westphalia the number of thefts reported to the police decreased

TABLE XXXIX. *German Federal Republic. Delinquency-rates per 100,000 Juveniles 14–18 of each Sex, 1948–52*

	Boys	*Girls*
1948	1,899	352
1949	1,528	280
1950	1,274	211
1951	1,771	230
1952	1,622	220

from 283,381 during the twelve months ending at 30 June 1948 to 169,333 during the next twelve-month period.[1] After the critical year of 1948 delinquency-rates for juveniles of ages between 14 and 18 decreased up to 1952 by 18 per cent. and thus surpassed the decrease in adult crime-rates which fell by only 12 per cent. The movement of delinquency-rates throughout the years 1948–52 shows, as indicated in Table XXXIX, the familiar late peak of 1951.[2] In the case of German juvenile delinquents, the rise in 1951 is the more remarkable for the conspicuous fall immediately preceding in 1950. However, the latter has been explained as the artificial result of an amnesty. The high delinquency-rates of 1951, which in the case of boys were above the figure for 1949, have been interpreted as a reflection of the 'Korea crisis' with its repercussions on the economy of the Federal Republic.[3] There is a further similarity in the trends of juvenile delinquency in England and in Germany. In both countries the recovery of recent years still leaves the delinquency-rates much higher than they had been before their spectacular increase under the impact of the Second World War. In England and Wales the delinquency-rate for junior boys was 1,122 in 1953 as compared with 798 in 1938, and for

[1] R. Jacobs, *Die Kriminalität der Nachkriegszeit in Deutschland*, 1952, p. 11.

[2] 6 *Wirtschaft und Statistik* (1954), 384–6.

[3] Jacobs, op. cit., p. 49; see also K. S. Bader, *Beobachtungen zur Nachkriegskriminalität* (1952), p. 9.

senior boys 1,663 in 1953 compared with 1,131 in 1938. Germany experienced twice in the lifetime of the present generation a complete economic disruption followed by a dramatic fresh start leading to new prosperity. In the year of the collapse of the German currency, 1923, the delinquency-rate for juveniles had risen to 1,082, to fall within two years to 489 in 1925. In 1948 it was as high as 1,137, but in 1950 it was with a figure of 752 still above the level it had reached two years after the liquidation of the crisis following the First World War. This upward trend in delinquency seems to be characteristic of juvenile lawlessness. Crime-rates of adults fell from 1,812 in 1923 to 1,311 in 1925, while after the Second World War they reached the conspicuous figure of 2,519 in 1948, but fell considerably below the 1925 level to 812 in 1950.[1]

These few comparative notes confirm, or at least illustrate, the general impression of a subsiding tide of juvenile delinquency. Nowhere are the figures by themselves negligible. However, the stormy fluctuations within a persistently upward trend seem to have come to a halt. A certain stabilization has apparently been reached at a level below the immediate post-war peaks.

At the time of the alarming rise in delinquency in 1948 and 1951, magistrates and educationalists were much concerned to find the causes of the increasing amount of juvenile misbehaviour. Today we seek an explanation of the apparent turning of the tide since 1951. It is difficult enough to define possible causes of delinquency in general or of its increase at a certain time and place. The accumulation of empirical knowledge about factors of crime and characteristics of offenders has not made this task easier. It appears, however, even more difficult to answer the question: Why *not* crime? or at least, Why less crime?

One may seek an explanation of these fluctuations in the changing circumstances in the life of different generations. The rise and fall of juvenile delinquency is determined by boys between 11 and 17 who always have the highest crime-rates. Those who belonged to this age group in 1953 had been born shortly before the war or during its first years. Although their early childhood was affected by the war, they spent their

[1] 6 *Wirtschaft und Statistik* (1954), 384–6.

school days under less disadvantageous conditions than their predecessors. While the older juveniles of 1953 went to school when the war was still going on, the educational system had already overcome the worst anomalies due to mass evacuation and the upheaval of the early war years. Another factor may be the return to normality in the economic life of the nation. With the end of rationing and with a full supply of consumer goods the temptation to steal scarce goods known to be in high demand disappeared and so did the possibility of finding a purchaser only too willing to take such things without asking questions. However, in this context a psychological factor ought not to be overlooked. The crime situation of a specific time cannot be ascertained with complete objectivity from statistical figures alone. The final assessment is a question of interpretation and this implies an unavoidable subjective element. The rising crime figures of the immediate post-war years coincided with a widespread feeling of insecurity in almost every sphere of life. The recent receding figures occur in a different climate of public opinion. Economic life appears to be more stabilized and prosperous. A number of bold long-term projects seem to point to a brighter future. As years go by, mankind has adjusted itself to the frightening picture of an unsettled peace. As an observation period the last two years of Criminal Statistics are too short to justify far-reaching conclusions. The figures alone do not tell us whether they represent a mere chance fluctuation or a true subsiding of the tide. The general assumption that the curve of delinquency is actually flattening out is in itself a symptom of a lessening strain and a growing confidence in the general feeling of popular opinion.

A study of criminal careers often leads to the disappointing impression that of all factors which influence the lives of delinquents the penal and corrective measures applied are the least effective. However, while it is very difficult to isolate the causative influence of treatment, it would be wrong to take an extreme view and to discard its possible effect altogether. In a discussion of the recent trend in juvenile delinquency in England and Wales, due attention must be given to new developments in the field of remedial and preventive measures. The period 1949–53 includes the first five years of the work of the Children's Officer whose functions have been established under the Children Act, 1948. The growing numbers under his care comprise two groups, those received, though not against the will of the parents, for lack of adequate parental care, and those committed by the juvenile court. On 30 November 1949 the number of all children under the care of Children's Officers was 55,255. Four years later, on 30 November 1953, it had risen to 65,309. While the majority of these children were received into the care of the Children's Officer with their parents' consent, voluntary cases and court cases contributed almost equal numbers to the increase of some 10,000 during the four-year period. The figures in Table XL show a considerable extension in the use of preventive measures both in the administrative and in the judicial sphere.[1]

TABLE XL. *Children under the Care of Children's Officers*

	30 Nov. 1949	*30 Nov. 1953*
Received into care with parents' consent . .	41,233	46,250
Committed by the courts .	14,022	19,059
TOTAL	55,255	65,309

In the light of the bare words of the statutory provisions the foregoing observations seem to suggest that the answer to family problems is first and foremost a separation of children from inadequate family homes. There are indeed cases where no other solution is possible, and these must be admitted to public care. At the same time, practical experience and psychological considerations have put a new emphasis on the indispensable educative functions of the natural family and thus made it clear how much the emotional and character development of a child is endangered by his early removal from the parental home. It is today universally accepted that all possibilities of maintaining the family unit must be exhausted before the Children's Officer or the juvenile court come to the conclusion that on balance the child's removal is necessary. The great achievement of voluntary social work since the war is the exemplary feat of the Family Service Units. As mentioned before, they supplement

[1] Figures taken from the *Sixth Report of the Work of the Children's Department*, 1951; *Children in Care of Local Authorities in England and Wales*, H.M.S.O., 1954, Cmd. 9145.

specialized case work in respect of individuals by comprehensive team-work to help problem families where the welfare of children is in danger. In Birmingham, where in 1952 no less than 554 children were received into public care, the Family Service Unit, while operating to a very limited extent only, has succeeded in keeping some 20–30 children in their own homes who otherwise would have had to be taken into the care of the Children's Officer.[1] Enlightened local authorities apply similar methods of family case work within the framework of statutory child care. The Children and Young Persons (Amendment) Act, 1952,[2] facilitates the intervention of the juvenile court for the benefit of ill-treated or neglected children who are exposed to unnecessary suffering or injury to health; but it also extends the power of the Children's Officer beyond a mere response to complaints by imposing on the local authority the duty to make inquiries whenever information points to the possibility of a juvenile being in need of care or protection. Such inquiries are made with a remedial purpose, as family case work with the aim of avoiding public intervention as far as possible.[3] There exists also the practice of licensing, under supervision, to their own parental home, children whom the juvenile court had committed to the local authority as a 'fit person'. In Birmingham, where in 1952 fifteen offenders and fifty-one non-offenders were committed to the care of the local authority under fit-person orders, there were at the end of the year twenty-four children licensed to their own parents. In the same year, twelve fit-person orders were revoked after a successful period of licence.[4] These practices have had the beneficial effect of bringing prevention to bear at an earlier stage. Not only is the individual child prevented from suffering and from succumbing to the influence of a bad home, but the family home is prevented from deteriorating to such an extent that the children must be taken away lest they are brought up below the standards which the community feels justified in tolerating.

The tendency to use certain legal forms of public action for more far-reaching preventive efforts is apparent in other fields

[1] *The First Four Years*, Report of the Children's Officer of the City of Birmingham, 1949–53, p. 19.

[2] 15 and 16 Geo. VI and 1 Eliz. II, c. 50.

[3] See, for a report on such work in Nottingham, *Manchester Guardian*, 15 Feb. 1955.

[4] Birmingham Report, op. cit., p. 32.

too. In Chapter III of this survey the relation between the traditional practice of police cautioning and the work of the juvenile courts has been discussed. In Liverpool, one of the high-delinquency areas, the usual practice of administering cautions to young law-breakers has been supplemented by the work of Juvenile Liaison Officers, appointed in June 1949 for this special full-time function in each of the seven divisions of the city. These officers were specially selected for their work with wayward and delinquent youth.[1] In one of the divisions the Juvenile Liaison Officer is described in a recent survey as a man 'who would immediately qualify for the category of social worker rather than of policeman'.[2] These officers have a wide discretion in their work for the prevention of juvenile delinquency. They perform an unofficial 'after-care' of juveniles cautioned by the police, they visit homes and meet there with increasing good will and co-operation from the parents, they call at multiple stores where managers prefer to let them deal informally with young pilferers rather than prosecute them, they are asked by headmasters and teachers to come and treat incidents which happened at school or came to the knowledge of the staff, and they introduce juveniles into clubs and other healthy spare-time activities. Besides these direct methods, they collect valuable experience about the personal circumstances of young offenders, about danger spots and opportunities for harmless leisure pursuits within the division, and they keep close contact with probation officers, youth leaders, and other social workers. In 1952, when in Liverpool 1,715 juveniles were found guilty before the magistrates, the Juvenile Liaison Officers dealt with 560 boys and 61 girls who had stolen, and 80 boys and 10 girls guilty of other offences. Out of this total of 711 juveniles, 51 committed subsequent offences up to March 1954. It has been claimed that this experiment in combination with further efforts in municipal and voluntary youth work contributed largely to the reduction of court figures in Liverpool which fell from 2,574 juveniles found guilty between April 1947 and March 1948 to 1,998 in the corresponding

[1] Liverpool City Police, *Juvenile Liaison Officers*, 1952; (Liverpool) *Report on the Police Establishment and the State of Crime for the Year 1952*, 1953.

[2] J. B. Mays, A Study of a Police Division, 3 *Brit. Journal of Delinquency* (1953), 185–97, at p. 188.

period of 1953–4.[1] The figures in Table XXXV suggest that the decrease of juvenile delinquency in Liverpool is mainly due to a drastic reduction in the number of junior boys. The total of boys of 8–13 found guilty of indictable offences fell from 1,314 in 1951 to 773 in 1953, a result which has no parallel elsewhere. It is highly probable that the work of the Liaison Officers is largely concentrated on these young schoolboys, but it would need further local investigations to find out how much this spectacular difference in the figures for 1951 and 1953 represents a true decrease in juvenile lawlessness beyond a mere, though in itself desirable, drop in the number of court cases. More recently, the city of Leeds has followed the Liverpool example and assigned Juvenile Liaison Officers to each of the four divisions.

In the field of penal and corrective measures, the enactment of the Criminal Justice Act, 1948, resulted in certain changes in the armoury of the courts. Corporal punishment was abrogated, the power of magistrates to commit a juvenile offender to prison as a punishment abolished, and two new measures introduced, attendance at an Attendance Centre and detention in a Detention Centre. The fact that they were instituted by the same Act which removed more serious penalties from the statute book indicates that the two new methods are designed for punitive purposes, but at the same time both are intended as forms of treatment which leave room for a constructive educative effort. In the past it has always proved very difficult to devise something which by its very nature combines such heterogeneous effects as deterrence and reformation. Only practical experience can show to what extent the two new measures will contribute to a successful reduction of juvenile delinquency. In 1950 the first three Attendance Centres for boys of 12 to 17 were opened, in London, at Smethwick (Staffordshire), and Hull. In these centres the three-hour attendance on any single one of the prescribed number of occasions is divided between fatigues like floor-scrubbing and constructive activities like handicrafts and first-aid instruction. It has been described as the aim of such treatment that the boys shall remain under firm discipline and should, at the same time, learn by experience the proper use of leisure so that a number of them may

[1] *News Chronicle*, 9 June 1954.

in the end find their way into a local youth organization.[1] A critical observer found it difficult to believe that such far-reaching educative aims can be achieved in a limited number of three-hour attendances with no opportunity for appealing to the boy's own initiative or sense of responsibility.[2] However, facilities for such compulsory attendance have considerably increased. In 1953 a total of 754 boys received attendance orders, among them 182 for simple and minor thefts, and a further 182 for burglary and house- or shop-breaking. By 1954 some thirty-two Attendance Centres had been established in England and Wales.

Like the Attendance Centre, the other new method, detention in a Detention Centre, has only begun to find its appropriate place within the present system of penal and corrective measures. The first Detention Centre for boys of 14 to 17 was opened on 25 August 1952. In 1953 210 boys were received, the majority for sentences of three months with a possibility of a fortnight's remission. The experience gained so far seems to suggest that previous moderate criminal experience does not exclude a fair prospect of success, but that boys who failed after a long-term institutional treatment, especially in an Approved School, are very likely to fail again after a short period of detention.[3] Both new measures are not intended to compete with either probation or Approved Schools. They fill the gap which exists in traditional treatment methods for dealing with those young offenders who, in view of their personal circumstances and social background, are not in need of a longer process of re-education, either extra-mural or institutional, but must be stopped by an impressive halt on an otherwise slippery slope from casual delinquency to persistent crime.

Among the innovations of the Criminal Justice Act, 1948, Remand Centres have not yet been established. This has the unfortunate effect that, against the intentions of the law-givers, juveniles are still committed to prison. In 1952 no less than 563 juveniles were received in prison in addition to 5 juvenile offenders sentenced to imprisonment by higher courts which

[1] *Sixth Report of the Children's Department*, p. 57.

[2] John Spencer, 1 *Brit. Journal of Delinquency* (1951), 230–2; 8 *Howard Journal* (1952), 146–8.

[3] *Report of the Commissioners of Prisons, 1953*, pp. 87–92; 5 *British Journal of Delinquency* (1955), pp. 190–209.

have still the power to do so. Out of the 563 juveniles committed to prison 319 boys and 31 girls were remanded in custody, 59 boys and 9 girls had to go to prison to await transfer to an Approved School, and 142 boys and 3 girls of 16 to await transfer to a Borstal Institution. Obviously, these prison committals of young people of juvenile court age are highly undesirable. In the words of an experienced prison administrator, they learn in prison a language which makes any subsequent corrective treatment even more difficult.

Obstacles to a successful preventive policy are found outside the administration of justice too. It would be wrong to regard Youth Clubs primarily as institutions for the prevention of juvenile delinquency. However, as an invaluable link in the sequence of forces which teach young men and women the art of living and good citizenship, they contribute to the building up of higher values and a better way of life than the short-lived pleasures gained by dishonesty and licence. Yet, social changes have affected the whole situation with which the clubs have to deal, and consequently altered the prospects of recruiting a new generation of club leaders. Sir Basil Henriques in summing up his experience has described the changes which have taken place. Forty years ago, it was the street urchin, starved of material things, who had to be provided with a better and more satisfactory way of life in the club, and for this task many willing hands could be found. Today it is the 'spiv', starved of things spiritual, who needs a genuine and convincing experience of personal fellowship and devotion, and this makes the task of finding the right type of club leader and helper more urgent and much more difficult.[1]

This brief account of recent developments in England and Wales shows a number of fresh preventive and remedial forces at work, but also certain impediments and obstacles still outstanding. Like the crime situation itself, the state of preventive policy and the facilities for treatment are the result of a coincidence of many different and sometimes divergent tendencies. Because of this, it has proved exceedingly difficult in the preceding discussion to assess the direct effect of one or the other variety of judicial treatment practice. Any statement in respect

[1] Sir Basil Henriques, 'Recruitment of Men at the Universities', Paper for private circulation (1954).

of certain types of juvenile offenders or any preference for one or the other form of treatment had to be made with due regard to all accompanying circumstances at the particular time and place. However, in the search for evidence on the direct effect of a certain way of treatment, one should not lose sight of the indirect influence of judicial treatment practice. To select the appropriate form of treatment is more than a mere technical question, and something which transcends in its importance the individual case. The spirit in which the juvenile court law is administered, the attitude which directs the choice of the measures applied, and the constant reappraisal of principles in the light of experience in respect of after-careers of former delinquents, are powerful forces which shape the climate of public opinion which in itself has a strong influence on success or failure in the treatment of juvenile delinquents.

INDEX OF PLACES AND DISTRICTS

Administrative counties are printed in capitals. All figures in respect of text and of tables refer to page numbers.

www.ingramcontent.com/pod-product-compliance
Ingram Content Group UK Ltd.
Pitfield, Milton Keynes, MK11 3LW, UK
UKHW021027041026
15470UKWH00013B/66

9 780313 201943